A Woman in Both Houses

A WOMAN IN BOTH HOUSES

MY CAREER IN NEW MEXICO POLITICS

Pauline Eisenstadt

Foreword by Jim Belshaw

University of New Mexico Press • Albuquerque

© 2012 by the University of New Mexico Press
All rights reserved. Published 2012
Printed in the United States of America
17 16 15 14 13 12   1 2 3 4 5 6

Library of Congress Cataloging-in-Publication Data

Eisenstadt, Pauline, 1938–
A woman in both houses : my career in New Mexico politics /
Pauline Eisenstadt ; foreword by Jim Belshaw.
     p. cm.
Includes index.

ISBN 978-0-8263-5024-4 (pbk. : alk. paper) — ISBN 978-0-8263-5025-1 (electronic)
 1. Eisenstadt, Pauline, 1938–
 2. Women legislators—New Mexico—Biography.
 3. Legislators—New Mexico—Biography.
 4. New Mexico. Legislature. House of Representatives—Biography.
 5. New Mexico. Legislature. Senate—Biography.
 6. New Mexico—Politics and government—1951–
 7. Women—Political activity—New Mexico.
 I. Title.

F801.4.E47A3 2012
328.73′092—dc22
[B]

                        2011015297

All images, unless otherwise noted, are courtesy of the author.

Dedicated to my grandchildren

> *Natalia, Paola, Spencer, and Holly, Eisenstadts all.*
> *At the end of the day I hope you will have*
> *great stories and no regrets.*

Contents

Foreword

By Jim Belshaw

B y turns entertaining, informative, and insightful, this memoir by one of
New Mexico's most astute political veterans finds wisdom taking numerous forms, not the least of which is humor, which Pauline Eisenstadt
tells us is a quality of great and lasting value. So let's look at what may be my
favorite moment in this marvelous memoir.

The year was 2009. Pauline and her husband, Mel, had lived in Corrales
since 1975. She held elective office for twelve years and had been involved
in community affairs for more than thirty years. On a Sunday, she and Mel
walked along the Rio Grande when they came upon a friend who was walking
with another woman.

Stopping to visit, Pauline's friend introduced the woman, identifying
Pauline by her full name—Pauline Eisenstadt.

The woman paused a moment and said, "I know that name."

She mulled this over another moment and said, "You used to be somebody."

Indeed, she used to be somebody.

She is the first woman to have served in both the New Mexico House and
Senate. Those years saw her working with four governors—two Democrats:
Bruce King and Toney Anaya; and two Republicans: Garrey Carruthers and
Gary Johnson.

In the House and Senate, she served with some of the most memorable
names in New Mexico political history—Manny Aragon, Raymond Sanchez,
Max Coll, and a host of others who need little or no introduction to those who
follow New Mexico politics closely or do nothing more than give the front
page of a newspaper a cursory glance. She was not only witness to a great deal
of New Mexico's political history, she was an active participant. She, in fact,
made much of that history herself.

Pauline Eisenstadt shares a wealth of experience and knowledge in this
book. On one level, it is a good read, engaging and lively, but it goes well
beyond that level and into another that is marked by understanding and good

judgment about where we have been and where we might go. While politics certainly play a major role in her look back over thirty years of community service, she instructs us in the art of governance, as well.

She begins each chapter with an epigraph from various historical figures to set the tone of the chapter. One stands out to me as setting the tone for the entire book as well as her long career. It comes from Vaclav Havel, former president of the Czech Republic: "Genuine politics is simply a matter of serving those around us: serving the community and serving those who will come after us. Its deepest roots are moral because it is a responsibility expressed through action to and for the whole."

Early on, she says it is her hope that this memoir will be of value to young people with political aspirations and that it will provide insight into how the system works or doesn't work in Santa Fe. She hopes the book will inspire people to become involved in their communities and to ensure that their leaders do their jobs with "honesty, integrity and always leavened with good humor." It succeeds in these and all the other goals she has set for herself in this memoir.

I have already mentioned one of those moments of good humor. There are more. There is the lesson learned on the House floor about how one might see a bill defeated simply by answering a call from Mother Nature at the wrong time.

She speaks of the moment in the Senate when Manny Aragon came to her to enlist help with two of his projects. The paper he held in his hand had three columns. Two came under headings identifying the projects. The third identified those people who had earned a spot on a particular kind of list he thought it best to avoid.

There is the lunch in Washington with Representative Harold "Mud" Runnels, who upon hearing that she opposes his stand on energy issues, inquires as to whether she is a "socialist." This is followed by a lunch hour lecture replete with graphs, charts, and notes scribbled on paper place mats.

The book is full of such moments. Pauline brings us to the floor of the House or Senate where we can see with intimacy and clarity how the governmental machinery operates—or doesn't. She takes us into the meeting rooms where much of the legislative work is done. We walk with her during campaigns, knocking on doors, compiling the nuts and bolts of a political campaign, the small details that will make the difference between victory and defeat.

Sound judgment makes appearances where one might not expect to find it—a flight of sandhill cranes, perhaps.

Reflecting on the dangers of power being concentrated in the hands of a few for too long, she came to believe that over the long haul it was best to see some of kind of rotation in that power so it was diffused instead of remaining in the same hands. She found herself thinking about this one day at home as she looked skyward and saw the familiar V-formation of migrating cranes overhead. She asked a biologist friend how the cranes chose a leader for those long flights every year.

She tells us: "He said they rotate the position because it is too hard on the leader to be in front too long. I have often thought the cranes have something to teach us about leadership and the need for change."

Like the cranes, Pauline Eisenstadt has something to teach us. She succeeds admirably.

Preface

During my dozen years in the New Mexico state legislature I have served with four governors and recent research has revealed that I am the first woman to have served in both the House and the Senate. That puts a smile on my face and reminds me of the honor I have had to serve as an elected official in our wonderful state of New Mexico, my chosen home.

It seems appropriate to begin this memoir with the assembling of the legislature in Santa Fe for the opening day of the legislative session. At the beginning of each session we would all assemble in the chamber of the House of Representatives to hear the State of the State address delivered by the governor in front of a packed chamber and gallery.

Opening day is the third Tuesday in January as established by the constitution, and there is a buzz in the air and usually it's very cold outside. The guests on the podium always include former governors, lieutenant governors, former legislators, former judges, present Supreme Court judges, and other dignitaries. The introductions are read by the clerk of the House and everyone is greeted with a round of applause. It resembles a big family reunion with lots of hugs and handshakes, and hopes are high for great accomplishments to follow in the legislative session that is beginning.

After all the stress and tension of the campaigns, this is a welcome beginning of a new session. All of the legislators had our families and friends sitting with us, and I would arrange for some of us to gather for lunch after all the speeches were finished. There was a lot of politicking, because it was our job to line up votes and support for our legislative issues. It is delightful to remember these days of hopeful beginnings, full of excitement and good cheer.

The governors' speeches would describe their key issues, their hopes for the session, and the ways they hoped to help New Mexicans have full and successful lives. These differed considerably as their attitudes toward the role of government were different.

Now, as I sit at my computer writing this memoir it is December 2009, and I am spending my time living in the past and trying to re-create the events in my life that led me on this journey that has put me in the New Mexico

House of Representatives and the New Mexico State Senate for a significant part of my life.

The definition of *memoir* that I like best is from the author Gabriel García Márquez. I have paraphrased his comments from Spanish: "Life is not what you lived, but what you remember and how you remember it."

As this memoir unfolds, I hope it will be of value to young people with political aspirations, provide some political insights about how the system works or doesn't work in Santa Fe, and inspire others to get involved and try to make sure that our leaders are doing their jobs with honesty, integrity, and always leavened with good humor.

Acknowledgments

The idea of doing a memoir began to bubble up into my consciousness as I was trying to decide what to do with the boxes of material that I had kept from my legislative career.

I'm the packrat in our family, and the dust was collecting and the space was becoming crowded. After conversations with the Center for Southwest Research at the University of New Mexico, I realized that my archives were worth saving.

Many friends began encouraging me to write a memoir and offered to help with the work and I thank you all. Jim Belshaw suggested I talk with the director of the University of New Mexico Press, Luther Wilson. I discussed the project with Luther, and he was encouraging and agreed to be my editor.

Five months later, after taking leave from all the boards of directors, formal and informal groups I belong to, the memoir is finished.

This memoir was accomplished with the help and encouragement of a number of people whom I wish to thank. My sons Todd and Keith as well as their wives Mireya and Kristy were enthusiastic about the project from the beginning. They suffered through a lot of my stories, laughed appropriately, and made valuable suggestions. Todd read and marked it up, like the professor he is, for useful changes. Keith sent suggestions always punctuated with enthusiasm for the memoir. My granddaughter Natalia, eleven years old, read the first chapter and immediately said, "You need some pictures." My sister Mickey Greenspan read the first half and told me how much she liked it, and my niece, Laurel Kaufer, also was complimentary.

I received research data from the Legislative Council Service in Santa Fe with the help of the librarian, Tracey Kimball. She also told me what a great contribution it would be for the history of the New Mexico legislature.

All of the epigraphs at the beginning of each chapter were taken from a book of readings and quotes called *At the End of the Day*, self-published in 2007 by Harriet and Alan Lewis, founders of Grand Circle Corporation, Kensington, New Hampshire. We have taken a number of European river trips with Grand Circle Travel and appreciate their philosophy of travel. The book reflects that we as humans have all confronted the same challenges and found strength in the same truths.

Frances Fanning interviewed ten of the people who helped me in early campaigns as volunteers and we continue to be friends today. These interviews provided inspiration for me as I wrote this memoir. Scott Alley was the reader for the University of New Mexico Press, and she told me later that there was nothing else like it in the literature, written by a former legislator. I want to thank Jim Belshaw for the foreword he wrote so beautifully and his kind encouragement.

My big thanks to Norris Tidwell, my friend and neighbor who was my computer guru. He helped when the "munchkins" got inside my computer and it no longer heard my commands. Without his calm ability to fix the problems I don't think I would have finished.

As a novice writer, it is important to keep the energy flowing, with the right amount of encouragement and criticism. My editor, Luther Wilson, had the right balance. He told me, "I will make suggestions, but this is your memoir, so you decide what you want to do." This relieved my anxiety a lot and enabled me to complete the task.

I've saved my biggest support system for last, my husband Mel Eisenstadt. Mel is a published author so he has been through the process of putting your thoughts and ideas on paper in a coherent and readable manner. He read each chapter as I finished it and proofed it for grammar, spelling, and coherence. He is considerably more accomplished than the "tools" on the computer.

Mel has been my partner and best friend for fifty years. He is a large part of my life's memories and has always told me, "You can do it, and I'll help you." Thank you, dear Mel.

Introduction

One generation plants the trees; another gets the shade.
—Chinese proverb

New Mexico is my home, and I have learned to appreciate so much about it. I love the diversity of the people and the landscape. We arrived here in 1973 so that my husband Mel could attend the University of New Mexico Law School, and my journey in the life of New Mexico public service and politics began.

We came here after living in Puerto Rico for three years, where my husband was a professor of engineering and I took care of our young sons and taught a few classes in English as a second language. We loved the island and its people, and we made some lifelong friends there as well as confirming our need to be near an ocean or water for parts of our lives. Our experience in Puerto Rico, with a Hispanic culture, prepared us only somewhat for our new home in New Mexico. The major similarity was the language, but the food, history, and culture of New Mexico are more similar to Mexico. However, one of the best things to come from our time in Puerto Rico was the comfort it provided for our sons in a different culture and language. Todd learned Spanish before he could read in English, and he was helping us maneuver in the language by the time he was in first grade. It was no surprise that he selected a wonderful woman named Mireya Solis from Mexico to marry. They live in Bethesda, Maryland, today.

Our son Keith joined the Peace Corps after college and spent time in a village in Paraguay, teaching in the high school and learning the language of Guaraní. Keith married an equally wonderful woman named Kristy Pilgrim, and they live in Missoula, Montana; I don't think he speaks much Guaraní there.

On arrival in New Mexico, we lived in Hoffmantown, near Indian School Road, for two years while my husband went to law school and I worked part time at the University of New Mexico for the Institute of Social Research on an education project. Three afternoons a week I tutored minority students for the

Title 9 program. This was a very busy time for our little family, but we learned a lot about Albuquerque and New Mexico.

After our marriage in 1960 in Miami Beach, Florida, we went to live in Tucson, Arizona, where my husband earned his PhD in mechanical engineering and I earned a master's degree in social sciences in education. I worked as a social worker our first year and taught high school during our last years there. There are some similarities between Tucson and Albuquerque, and we acquired our affection for chile and the Hispanic culture in Tucson. I taught at Pueblo High School, with students who were from families that had been in my caseload from the welfare department. I learned compassion and understanding of how difficult it was for some children to concentrate on school work when they didn't have enough to eat and were sleeping with two others in the same bed at home.

I am optimistic by nature and temperament, and I'm always willing to try something new. That aspect of my personality enabled me to adapt and adjust to our new surroundings and also helped me look at the big picture wherever we located during our early years.

In 1965 the University of California, Santa Barbara, hired my husband to teach in the Department of Mechanical Engineering, and we spent five years there. Both of our sons were born there, and after staying home with our first son, I realized that I needed to utilize my education and took a part-time job at the University of California working for a group of psychologists. At the same time, I read Betty Friedan's book entitled *The Feminine Mystique*, and it led me to think differently about my role and my future. In my generation, women were expected to stay home and raise the children. My friends in California were all educated, had worked, and were now home with the children. Once the kids were in school they all began to work again, as did I.

A memoir conveys memories of a part of your life, and this one will focus on my public service and political career. However, it seems to me that it would be of interest to understand my career, so journey with me to my origins. That will take me back to another part of my life in Florida, where my family moved when I was ten months old. My mother and father, Anne and Morris Bauman, moved to Florida from New York, with my beloved older sister, Marilyn and myself.

Growing up in Miami Beach, Florida, in the 1940s and 1950s has left me with lots of wonderful memories. My sister Marilyn (later Mickey) and I went to Central Beach Elementary School, Ida M. Fisher Junior High, and Miami Beach Senior High School, which were always within walking or bicycling distance of our home. We were also always within walking distance of the beach, and we often spent the weekends meeting with friends all day long on our special "hangout beaches" of Fourteenth Street or Forty-first Street. My sister

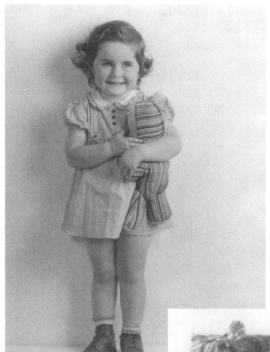

⊛ Pauline Bauman Eisenstadt,
two and a half years old.

⊛ Marilyn Bauman Greenspan, four years old;
Pauline Bauman Eisenstadt, one and a half
years old.

✪ Pauline—high school graduation, 1956.

was three and a half years older, so she always had to take me with her when we were young, and I expect she tired of that. But she didn't complain, and as we got older we became best friends. We return to Florida yearly to visit my sister and her husband Sid Greenspan. They now live in Ft. Lauderdale as does their daughter, Sherra Payne, and her family. My other niece, Laurel Kaufer, and her family live in Los Angeles, California.

I always return to visit Miami Beach. However, it is now the home of the Art Deco revival and the area has become a magnet for very wealthy people living in high rise condos from all over the world. We loved growing up there, but we had no idea that the architecture of the hotels was so special or that it would one day become such an exclusive place to live.

Our schools were all attached in one building and I went to school with the same friends from kindergarten through high school. My high school was later moved as the population had moved farther north, but the elementary school is still there, and we've visited it on our most recent trip. Miami Beach Senior High School Alumni Association established a hall of fame, and I was inducted in 2000, the second year of its existence. It is interesting that Mark Medoff, the playwright, who was a professor at New Mexico State University, was inducted the same year as I was. We went to the same Miami Beach Senior High School; he graduated a few years after I did. Also, that same year Andy Garcia, the actor,

○ My sister's engagement party with my father,
Morris Bauman, and myself, 1957.

○ Graduation at the University of
Florida, 1960.

○ Graduation, with my father wearing my cap
and gown, with my mother Anne Bauman.

✪ Mel and I at our wedding at the Eden Roc Hotel in Miami Beach, Florida, 1960. Courtesy of Werner Kahn Studio.

was inducted and two members and friends were inducted a year earlier: Robert Rubin, President Clinton's secretary of the treasury, and Skip Bertman, winning baseball coach for Louisiana State University. My high school had a very high percentage of graduates that went to college, about 85 percent.

In 1960 I went to the University of Florida in Gainesville and really enjoyed the comprehensive courses, or "C courses," of the first two years, which required that everyone take sciences, math or logic, English, humanities, art, and music before you went on to your major classes. My husband was an engineering student but he took all of the C classes too, and we both think that it was a wonderful way to be exposed to a lot of information and ideas that have lasted us a lifetime. I liked history, biology, geology, philosophy, economics, and humanities classes.

I had a good time at college. My sister was there my first year and she was a founder of a sorority, Delta Phi Epsilon, and so I followed in her footsteps again and joined the sorority.

The Gator football team at the University of Florida was always a big attraction, as were the parties afterward. I was a good athlete in junior high school intramural sports, but when I got to high school there were no competitive sports for girls and we were expected to become cheerleaders. Fortunately, that

○ Pauline, mother Anne, and sister Mickey in
Corrales, New Mexico, 1975.

changed when Congresswoman Patsy Mink of Hawaii required that women's sports be established at universities for them to receive federal funds. I have noticed that there are many girls' teams now that compete in basketball, softball, volleyball, swimming, and gymnastics at the high school and the university levels. Such sports were not available in my generation, and I'm so glad they are for my granddaughter's generation.

I graduated in 1960 with a bachelor of education in social sciences, married Mel, and we moved to Tucson, Arizona, where we both went to graduate school. I worked during the day, teaching high school, and went to the University of Arizona at night for two years and graduated with a master's degree in social sciences. I was pregnant with our first son when we relocated to Santa Barbara, California, when Mel was hired by the University of California to teach in the mechanical engineering department.

A lot of my drive and ambition came from my parents. They were very hard workers and lived the American dream of immigrants achieving success in the United States. My parents worked hard, without having a higher education, by using their intelligence and energy. Like farmers and ranchers on the frontier of New Mexico, they survived by sweat and wit. They used the skills they had and started with a small sandwich shop and graduated to small apartment hotels in Miami and later Miami Beach. During World War II there was a lot of business activity in South Florida. My parents succeeded with a great deal of energy, hard work, honesty, and integrity, and they instilled this in my sister and me. They also expected us to do well and make a contribution to the larger community.

✪ Sons Keith, eight years old, and Todd, eleven and
a half years old. Corrales, New Mexico, 1978.

They also instilled a lot of confidence in us. My mother always told me that I could achieve anything I was prepared to do; she thought I could become the president of the United States. This, of course, was an exaggeration, but my mother was so proud when she attended the opening session of my second year at the House of Representatives. Children need lots of encouragement and love to grow into productive members of our society, and I always had a lot of both.

I have a strong sense of social justice and concern for equal opportunity for all that I received from my parents and our Reform Judaism religious background. I introduced and passed legislation concerning hate crimes in the New Mexico Senate and House that was vetoed by Governor Gary Johnson. This legislation was passed under Governor Bill Richardson, after I had retired in the year 2000.

I am no longer the same person I was when I first entered the public service arena in 1977. My memories may be different than others of the same incident, and of course, time does cloud the clarity of the past. I have one little story to tell that will conclude this introduction. We have lived in Corrales, New Mexico, a little village northwest of Albuquerque near the Rio Grande, since 1975. I've held elective office for a dozen years and been involved in the community for more than thirty years. One Sunday in September 2009, my husband and I were walking on the ditch bank of the river, when a friend came by, and we stopped to visit. She introduced me to her friend as Pauline Eisenstadt. The friend paused and said, "I know that name," and then she paused again and said, "You used to be somebody." With that comment and a smile of humility, I will begin my memoir.

CHAPTER ONE

The Changing Role of Women

Life shrinks or expands in proportion to one's courage.

—Anaïs Nin

The women's movement was born of the broader civil rights movement but it did not become the focus until later. The 1960s and 1970s, when the social conscience of many of my generation matured, was a time of turmoil in the United States on university campuses with the student population, particularly because of the war in Vietnam. Sex, drugs, and rock and roll seem to be the chapter heading for some, and they not only divided our country, but they also changed the norm for behavior in our generation. I was born in December 1938, just before the baby boom, after the depression was coming to an end and World War II was beginning. Lives were in upheaval, with the men at war leaving the women to take over jobs in industry, government, farms, and ranches. Once the women of our parents' generation took over and learned that they could do the work, they were not as content staying at home and in the kitchen anymore.

Our sons were born in Santa Barbara, California, in 1965 and 1969, and I had joined the American Association of University Women and the League of Women Voters, both active groups for women interested in studying the issues of importance for our communities and our country. The time was full of conflict as the students on the campus of the University of California, where Mel was teaching engineering, protested the war and got arrested. The student area of Isla Vista was under a curfew, and one night we got a call from our babysitter, who had been jailed as a protester and released in the middle of the night. Since her friends lived in Isla Vista, they could not leave to pick her up. Mel went to pick her up, and in the morning we had four students sleeping on our floor. Todd was three years old, and as he stepped over their bodies on his way to watch *Captain Kangaroo*, he asked, "Who are these people?" We were also conflicted about the war in Vietnam and upset when we received a note from Todd's preschool saying that if the preschool at the Presbyterian Church was teargassed we could pick him up at an alternative location. It was time to find a quieter place to live. Mel had gone to graduate school with two friends from Puerto Rico, and they had always asked him to come to Puerto Rico and teach engineering at the University of Puerto Rico in Mayaguez.

Puerto Rico has a Hispanic culture, and the role of women was different than on the mainland. We were referred to as "Continentals" because we were not native Puerto Ricans and that always set us apart. While living in a different culture the values of your own culture are magnified. The role of women and men and the relationship to the society was quite different in the Latin society. I attended a consciousness raising group, composed of other Continental women, and we discussed the issues of the women's movement that were being discussed simultaneously in small groups all over the United States.

These issues are still current but tremendous changes have taken place. Women now have a better opportunity to get into professional schools such as law school and medical school, receive equal pay for equal work, and not just running other people's campaigns but actually running for office, as I did. The young women of today do not describe themselves as feminists, because the term brings up the idea of "bra burners" and angry women from my generation. I was and am a feminist. The term to me means that women should be able to sit in any chair of leadership in politics, education, business, government, or at home, if they wish and are qualified. A woman should not be prohibited from achieving her highest goal because of her gender.

This is my hope for my three granddaughters and all of the other young women in our state, country, and the world.

When we arrived in New Mexico, I got two jobs and started to think about the changing roles of women. I asked Barbara Allender, who I had met at the Albuquerque League of Women Voters, if she would join me in preparing a grant for the New Mexico Humanities Council to organize forums on the "Changing Role of Women" around New Mexico. This began my understanding of the different parts of our state as we received a small grant and staged forums in about five locations, including Taos, Farmington, and Albuquerque, and a couple of others. This was 1974, and we found that there was a great deal of interest in the changing role of women among women all around the state. This was the same year that the Equal Rights Amendment was being debated in the state legislature of New Mexico. I recall going to the capitol to advocate for this along with many female lawyers, judges, students, working women, and many men. The Equal Rights Amendment vote was a very close vote in New Mexico, but it passed. I noticed that there were very few women in the seats of power who had the vote on this issue. This is the perfect example of why we need more women in elective office, because it makes a big difference in all of our lives to have women sitting at the table.

Years later, while I was sitting at my seat on the floor of the New Mexico State Senate, one of my friends on the floor of the Senate came over and congratulated me. I asked him why and he said "because you are the first and only woman to serve in both the House of Representatives and the Senate." That was in 1999, and we were all given a copy of a booklet called "New Mexico Women Legislators from 1923 to 1999" written by Dan D. Chavez and printed by the New Mexico Legislative Council Service for the purpose of historical legislative research. It didn't seem like much at the time, but I guess everyone likes to be a game changer because it opens up new possibilities for others. It provides an example for others to also follow if they wish.

My friend, Linda Lovejoy, served with me in the House and now she is also in the Senate, so I am not the only one to serve in both houses anymore, just the first. The Senate was more fun for me, and I will discuss this later, but doing both gave me a better understanding of how it all works for the state of New Mexico.

The 1911 constitution gave New Mexico women the right to vote and run for only three offices: school board member, county school superintendent, and school director. After the adoption of the women's suffrage amendment to the U.S. Constitution in 1920, all American women were given the right to vote for all elective offices, but the amendment did not give women the right to run for all public offices.

Women did not have the right to run for all public offices in New Mexico until an amendment to Section 2 of Article VII of the state constitution was ratified by the New Mexico voters in the special election of September 20, 1921. The vote tally was 26,744 votes for the amendment and 19,751 votes against the amendment. The vote was not an overwhelming endorsement for change, but changes in cultural patterns and behavior are always difficult and cause a "close vote."

The first woman legislator and woman state representative was Bertha M. Paxton, Democrat, who served one two-year term from 1923 to 1924, representing Doña Ana County. The first woman elected to the state Senate, Louise Holland Coe, Democrat, was first elected in 1924. Senator Coe served from 1925 to 1940 from Lincoln and Otero counties, Socorro County, and Torrance County. She is the only woman to date who has held the position of president pro tempore. She tried in 1940 to be the Democratic Party nominee for the U.S. House of Representatives but was not selected. After Coe's term ended in 1940, no woman served in the state Senate until 1965.

I wish I could have met these first women who were willing to integrate our political system and change the world in Santa Fe. We do indeed stand on the shoulders of these early women and walk in their skirts, because they created a new path for all of us to try to make better policy decisions that includes both genders and all the diverse population groups in New Mexico.

CHAPTER TWO

Back to School

Do not go where the path may lead. Go instead
where there is no path and leave a trail.
—Ralph Waldo Emerson

In 1976, we were living in Corrales, New Mexico, a rural village on the Rio Grande, twenty miles from Albuquerque. Our sons were in elementary school and I was ready for a new adventure. I was involved in our family business of investing and managing property but that enabled me to have time to do other activities. In our family when there was a transition or a fork in the road, we usually picked education as the new direction to follow. My new adventure would be going back to graduate school to study at the University of New Mexico for a doctorate in American Studies. My plan was an interdisciplinary course in sociology, English, and anthropology focusing on community studies. As I was an older graduate student of thirty-four years, I knew what I wanted to focus on in my studies and research. I began taking classes in the areas I was interested in studying. I did well and finished my coursework and language requirement, and then I needed a professor who would guide my dissertation research in this interdisciplinary field of community studies.

I had begun my research and was using the Village of Corrales as my study area. I researched the Private Land Claims Court Case of 1892, did an analysis of the 1870 federal census data of Corrales, and utilized data from an unpublished dissertation written by Paul Alfred Francis Walter Jr. in 1938. The major portion of the research consisted of oral histories obtained by interviewing descendants of the Spanish, Italian, and French families that adapted to the Spanish culture, and the latest Anglo, English-speaking arrivals to Corrales. I felt that it was important to capture the essence of this community through the voices of the "old-timers" in Corrales.

In the early times, a few relatively wealthy ranchers controlled the bulk of the Spanish land base. For instance, Captain Juan Gonzalez, who played the role of *patron*, or boss, for the community, probably ran large herds of sheep and cattle on the range land in 1712.

Margaret Mead points out that the patrons achieved leadership through financial status, knowledge of the outside world, or personal power. She records that in the more eastern villages of New Mexico, where there were no glaring inequalities of wealth, the patron principle was less clear. Mead states, "Throughout the structure of Spanish American society in New Mexico, authority and responsibility for leadership, power and obligation for dependents tends to focus on one person. There are no voluntary associations here, with elected leaders. Society is characterized by already present units: the paternalistic kinship group, the village with which it may prove to be coextensive. Within this, in the appropriate position, the patron rises in authority."

After the annexation of New Mexico by the United States, the patron became also a "jefe politico," or political boss, who could unfailingly deliver the county or precinct vote.

In my research I interviewed the people living in Corrales, finding out about the rhythm of their lives. The occurrences of great events in the world, such as world wars, were found beside the planting of apple orchards, important to the community of Corrales. This is the irony and the reality of living in small communities; a paved road has as much effect on that community as a larger world event. In small rural communities, such as Corrales, in the past there were "Dias de Mas" and "Dias de Menos," days of plenty and days of want. Life was dependent on farming and its seasonal cycle.

The evidence indicates that this is no longer true. Corrales has integrated with the larger community of Albuquerque, and it appears as if it will continue to change in that direction in the future, as the land value for residences has made it unprofitable to farm.

This research was concluded in 1977 and self-published in 1980 by Cottonwood Printing. The title is *Corrales, Portrait of a Changing Village* by Pauline Eisenstadt and illustrated by Lillian Kellogg. The book is a small glimpse into the village up to the time it was published and it is still quite popular, having gone through three printings.

With the Corrales Historical Society, a Corrales friend, Mary P. Davis, has just published a book called *Images of America, Corrales* (Arcadia Publishing, 2010) that is a collection of photographs depicting the old families and the lives they lived, which provides a great addition to our historic knowledge of Corrales.

When my classwork was finished, I began to realize that I enjoyed being out in the community and interacting with people, learning from them and working with them. I did not achieve my goal of a doctorate as I was losing interest in completing the dissertation. I wanted to be more involved in the actions of our community and have an input in the outcome of policy decisions. The life of an academic seemed less appealing to me, and I moved on with the next phase of my life.

I had learned a great deal about the Hispanic culture and how it functioned in little communities all over the state of New Mexico, and I began to understand the pattern of leadership, referred to as the "patron system." This became valuable to me as a politician and community volunteer and helped me understand how the legislature functioned on the Democratic side of the aisle.

There were a lot more Hispanics than Anglos in the Democratic Party in the House of Representatives and the Senate during my tenure from the 1980s through the 1990s. I was the only Anglo woman when I chaired the caucus for the Democrats in the House of Representatives, and I understood the leadership patterns better because of my research and study of small Hispanic communities in New Mexico.

CHAPTER THREE

How I Got into Politics

Think big and your deeds grow;
Think small and you'll fall behind;
Think that you can and you will—
It's all in the state of mind.

—Walter Wintle

My political career in New Mexico began with a consumer group I helped start in 1977 called Energy Consumers of New Mexico. The impetus for the group was the rising cost of heating oil for low-income people, seniors, and farmers pumping with natural gas for irrigation, and businesses that used quantities of natural gas. The cost was skyrocketing, and our group was formed to lobby the legislature to put a cap on the price charged for natural gas by the utility company. I worked part time as director, and Pat White, a friend from the League of Women Voters who had studied energy, was assistant director. We would arrive at the capitol in Santa Fe, sometimes with citizen volunteers, and lobby the legislature. I remember walking around the Roundhouse with Reverend F. W. Wells, an African American Baptist minister from Hobbs, who was an activist for his people on utility issues, and Johnny Thomas, a farmer from Estancia Valley, who also had a PhD in agriculture. It must have been a sight to see because we were such novices, and so sincere and so eager to talk to the people in legislature we thought could help us.

Attorney General Toney Anaya became our ally. He told us he was also concerned about the people of the state and their inability to pay their bills for heating during the winter. There were a number of legislators who also were willing to help our efforts. I learned later in my career that the real conflict for a gas-producing state, like New Mexico, is that the state budget benefits from higher prices for natural gas while the citizens of the state pay higher costs for their usage. The solution in these kinds of problems is usually a balance between the two, which necessitates advocates on each side to create the balance. We promoted the consumer advocate side and did a lot of public awareness through free media, interviews, press conferences, and meetings. We had some success and then we moved in a new direction suggested to me by former state senator and gubernatorial candidate Fabian Chavez. He said, "Pauline, go over to the Public Utility Commission and intervene in the utility cases." We began to focus on these issues, but that required money to pay lawyers to intervene in the cases. My role became that of marketing and development director, and grant getter in Washington.

Suzann Owings became my assistant director. We had met at the University of New Mexico in graduate school, and she was a talented person who helped a lot as the change in direction for Energy Consumers occurred. Susan Williams wrote a grant proposal that provided funding during the last year of Energy Consumers. My last assistant was a capable person, the late Ellen Feder Roth. She went on to teach elementary school for twenty-five years.

By 1983 it became time to select new leadership for Energy Consumers of New Mexico, and we selected Danice Picraux to be the next director. Danice Picraux is now a member of the House of Representatives of New Mexico and has had a long distinguished career since our days as early consumer advocates.

During my tenure with Energy Consumers of New Mexico our lawyers helped on cases at the Utility Commission, and they made a difference in the outcome of many cases benefiting the consumers. Noelle L'Homedieu wrote the brief that enabled the commission to take Public Service Company's Lear Jet airplane out of the rate base. It was not a legitimate cost for the ratepayers, and we all knew and understood that. Sudeen Kelly wrote consumer protection guidelines for the commission that provided direction for the rights of the ratepayers about things such as cutoff timetables, budgeting payments to prevent cutoffs of utility service, and other issues regarding proper procedures for the utilities and consumers to function with each other.

Mel Eisenstadt and Steve Schoen, as well as our two lawyers mentioned above, entered into the rate cases representing the consumer side of the equation. The team of lawyers working in the attorney general's Office of Consumer Affairs was also effective, and there were others representing Kirtland Air Force Base, a big user of gas and electricity, and large industrial users. All of these groups would work together in the first phase of the case, which was concerned with how much money the utility would make. Phase 2 was about the rate to be paid by each consumer group, and the groups would then split into residential and large business users to compete with each other in the case. The commission had to split the baby, so to speak, using the wisdom of King Solomon to decide how to fairly allocate costs to each group.

These are difficult decisions and fortunately the commission had thoughtful members that were appointed by governors Apodaca and King. The chairman was "Dickie" Montoya, and members Eileen Grevey (later Hillson) and Gary Blakely. The executive director was David Cohen, a good lawyer with calm temperament. He provided direction to the staff. Energy Consumers participated in cases on behalf of the consumers, and it was a very lively time and place for all of us. Looking back, I realize how difficult these decisions were, but how important it was for us to be there and present the consumer side.

During this time I was appointed as a member of the Consumer Advisory Committee of the now defunct Federal Energy Administration by Jack O'Leary, the deputy director who had worked in New Mexico as the secretary of energy and natural resources for Governor Apodaca.

I was also elected to the National Center of Appropriate Technology. That organization had headquarters in Butte, Montana, because Senator Mike Mansfield of Montana sponsored the enabling legislation. This was an organization created by the Federal Community Services Administration to serve low-income people through use of appropriate technology such as solar greenhouses, house plans for insulation, alcohol fuels, biomass, and others.

The following are excerpts from a journal that I had kept in 1982 about my work in Washington on national committees and marketing for our advocacy work on behalf of low-income people and the elderly. I called this section "A Citizen's View of Washington."

> I've been going to Washington on a regular basis for the past six years. Trips to Washington, whatever their stated purpose are always coupled with efforts to raise money through leads about potential sources for grants to effectively work on our issues. I would go to the meetings and then stay a few extra days on a friend's couch to try to locate some agency that had some money for our purposes. The money sources rest on Capitol Hill and whether you have programs like solar energy for everyone or subsidies for the defense industry, the pivotal place is on the Potomac.
>
> When President Carter created the Department of Energy, Secretary James Schlesinger appointed me to be the first chairwoman of the Department of Energy Consumer Advisory Committee. When serving on national advisory committees the major ingredient must be a sense of tenacity and humor. There were thirty-five members, representing all types of consumers: minorities, seniors, low income, handicapped, and others. We had briefings by Department of Energy officials and passed resolutions regarding the consumer impacts of the energy legislation.

We had a number of activist types on our committee, people who ran movements in their own states. We also had the president of Sun Oil on our committee, and he was always trying to understand our positions on issues. Our group was having dinner at a Greek restaurant, and I told Harlan Snider, president of Sun Oil, that I thought eventually the oil barons would become irrelevant. He asked me to come to Houston and tell the marketing vice presidents of all the oil companies the same thing. That is another story, as I did go to Houston and stay at the Sheraton with the key to the top floors, and had the Saudi Arabian newspaper served with coffee and rolls in the lobby every morning.

The resolution that caused the greatest furor was the one that recommended the Department of Energy investigate and study the cost effectiveness of nationalizing the oil industry. The repercussions of that were heard for five years afterward. I don't think anyone on the committee really believed that that was possible or even desirable, but we did know that the price of oil was controlled by OPEC, the cartel of the oil producing nations. The consumer in the United States was not protected from the greed and ability of the oil companies to raise the prices of gasoline and heating oil, in order to maintain and increase their profits. These problems are still with us, but perhaps the push for alternative energy will help alleviate the dependence of our economy on oil. The world's awareness of the global climate change caused in part by carbon dioxide may revolutionize the energy industry, and the oil barons may indeed become irrelevant. I wonder if my old friend, Harlan Snider, the president of Sun Oil is still alive to witness these possible changes.

On one of my first trips to Washington in 1978, I went to see Congressman Harold Runnels of New Mexico about the effect of gas deregulation on consumers. We talked for about thirty minutes, and then it was lunch time. Runnels asked me to join him in the congressional dining room with Congressman Manuel Luján, whom he called "Lujohn." Congressman Runnels drew diagrams on the paper place mat all through lunch. When I didn't agree that natural gas deregulation was good for New Mexicans because the price would rise considerably, he asked if I was a socialist. I told him no, and he proceeded to lecture me on free enterprise capitalism and how he never went to college and he was a millionaire. I was too new to the environment and too insecure to really enjoy the moment to its fullest. Halfway through lunch Congressman Luján joined us to finish me off, so to speak. He had a kind solicitous manner and is a gentleman of the old school, which was appreciated by this feminist.

Congressman Luján was my congressman and during our conversation we talked about his congressional voting record, which included voting against a lot of programs that would have helped the people in our district. When I asked him about that, he said, "I feel differently and my only purpose is to help my constituents." Congressman Luján then escorted me from the dining room through the labyrinth of the Capitol basement to the street level, where he hailed me a taxi and asked me to visit again soon. Needless to say, that was a heavy dose of Washington. I realized I had been lobbied by two of the best. Later that year Senator Pete Domenici's office requested that I give testimony on consumer positions before the Senate Energy Committee on the deregulation of natural gas. Much to the surprise of many consumers in New Mexico, Governor Toney Anaya's representative gave testimony in favor of deregulation because of the increased revenue this would generate since New Mexico is a producing state. This is a conundrum for New Mexico, and when I went to the legislature I began to see the larger picture; however, the balance between the state revenue and the consumers in New Mexico needs to be carefully focused.

Power is the name of the game in Washington. The rise and fall of centers of power is very quick. The ability to accomplish any worthwhile goal is the access to these power centers. The role of the citizen, as an individual, is not very large unless that citizen represents a constituency or possesses a great deal of wealth or influence. A year later, after I had won my first elective office as a state representative, I found that Santa Fe functions much like Washington, on a much smaller scale.

CHAPTER FOUR

Democratic National Convention
San Francisco, 1984

Genuine politics is simply a matter of serving those around us:
serving the community and serving those who will come after us.
Its deepest roots are moral because it is a responsibility
expressed through action, to and for the whole.

—Vaclav Havel

In 1984, I had just returned from San Francisco where I was a Gary Hart delegate to the Democratic National Convention. It was indeed a most exciting experience that I will long cherish.

The process began early, as the state convention selected delegates to the convention on June 9, after a lot of campaign effort on behalf of our candidates. The delegates were selected using a formula that reflected each candidate's strength at our state convention.

I was selected by the New Mexico delegation for Gary Hart to represent them on the National Democratic Party Platform Committee. I attended a meeting in Washington on June 20–24, and the representatives of all the presidential candidates fashioned a platform that tried to make a statement they could all support, prior to the convention the following month (on July 14, 1984, a date I remember because it is my son Keith's birthday).

The chairwoman of the Platform Committee was Congresswoman Geraldine Ferraro. She was widely acclaimed as having great ability, tenacity, and charm. I talked with her about the possibility of her nomination as the vice president, but she said she was too involved in all these other activities to think about it. She was the kind of person who you meet and immediately feel as if you have known for a long time. She was forthright, open to discussion of new ideas, and quite talented in the politics of accommodation for the proceedings of the Platform Committee. I introduced an issue about education for Native Americans, supported the Peace Academy and Puerto Rican self-determination, and participated on the Foreign Affairs Task Force. It was very exciting for me as all of the major presidential campaigns had their staffs at the table, and I was sitting with people that I had only read about or seen on television. There are often fights within the party about these platforms so they do reflect the issues of concern to the Democrat Party voters. I have served on the State Central Committee for the New Mexico Democratic Party and the Platform Committee. The candidates for governor run their own campaigns, but they do reflect the major directions of the party platforms. On some issues they may differ and then the party faithful have their own decisions to make about how they will vote for the candidates, but the platforms are a guide and the candidates try to prevent the capture of these committees by any extremist faction of the party.

The convention in San Francisco was not full of surprises as the major decisions on the platform had been decided, the major candidates had both supported Geraldine Ferraro as their vice presidential choice, and there was no great outpouring of demonstration against existing Democratic policy. My candidate, Gary Hart, had been damaged by a scandal concerning his activities with a woman who was not his wife, on a boat in Florida called *Monkey Business*. He was not able to recover from that publicity and his own recklessness.

We knew Vice President Mondale was the apparent winner for the nomination but Moscone Center was full of rumors up until the final vote about the first ballot being inconclusive. The major potential group that could threaten a first ballot nomination was the Hispanics because they wanted Mondale to take a stronger negative position on the Simpson-Mazoli Immigration Bill. The Hispanic caucus met and some members suggested abstention on the first ballot, but the majority voted against that and there were only about thirty-five abstentions.

The big events of the convention were the championship oratory of Governor Mario Cuomo, Reverend Jesse Jackson, Senator Ted Kennedy, Senator Gary Hart, Vice President Mondale, and Representative Geraldine Ferraro. These speakers stirred the hearts of the delegates, and there were floor demonstrations and outpourings of emotion from the entire convention. The historic nomination of Geraldine Ferraro, the first woman to be nominated as a vice presidential candidate, was exhilarating for me and all the other women on the floor of that convention in 1984. Hillary Clinton has come the closest to giving us a woman at the top of our political ticket in the United States, but I think that Geraldine Ferraro got us started in the direction of visualizing that possibility. She would have been a great vice president.

The New Mexico delegation was a small, close-knit group of twenty-eight delegates, nine alternates, spouses, a few children, and other state officials. Among the delegation were Governor Toney Anaya, Lieutenant Governor Mike Runnels, Senator Jeff Bingaman, Congressman Bill Richardson, Secretary of State Clara

Jones, State Democratic Chairman Fred Mondragon, Vice Chairwoman Bea Castellano, National Committee Woman Zora Hesse and her husband Frank Hesse, my husband Mel Eisenstadt, our friend Jay Sorenson, and many others that I had worked with on campaigns and would continue to do so in the future.

We caucused early every morning at 7:30 a.m., discussed platform issues, details about delegation passes needed for other scheduled events, and a general sharing of activities. There were caucuses for every interest group: environmental, nuclear freeze, women, Hispanics, blacks, and a lot of fringe groups. We all attended those that we were interested in and tried to juggle these with breakfast meetings, bus schedules to Moscone Center, and spouse interests as best we could. In addition to the attention to serious issues, there were parties of historic proportions, as San Francisco outdid itself with hospitality. Mayor Diane Feinstein hosted a four-story party in the rotunda of the city hall that was my choice for the classiest party I'd ever attended up to that time. There was a variety of food on each level: Italian, Chinese, seafood, Mexican, and everything else that California had to offer at that time. Everywhere the California vintners had spigots of red or white California wine. There was music everywhere, with violinists playing stereophonic music on every balcony.

A huge staircase with a red carpet soon filled up with magnificent choral voices singing patriotic songs, and white-gloved dancers, firecrackers, confetti and balloons from the rafters all contributed to a crescendo of good feeling and foot-tapping joy at our good fortune for being in San Francisco. My husband and I have traveled all over the world since that time and San Francisco continues to be one of our favorite places.

We all worked hard, sat on the convention floor, raised our voices in cheers for our candidates, and came home tired but exhilarated, hoping that our efforts would be the historic choice for the next president and vice president of the United States. History shows that we did not win that election, and it wasn't until 1992 that Bill Clinton won an election that put a Democrat in the White House again.

I came home and made the decision to run for election to the New Mexico House of Representatives.

CHAPTER FIVE

Political Campaigns

You gain strength, courage and confidence by every
experience in which you really stop to look fear in the face.
You must do the thing which you think you cannot do.

—Eleanor Roosevelt

I loved campaigning in the fall because it was harvest season, and I was fortunate to have a lot of small communities along the Rio Grande, starting
with Corrales, Bernalillo, Algodones, Peña Blanca, Sandia Pueblo, and
Santa Ana Pueblo in my legislative district. In the fall, starting in Corrales, the
smell of fresh roasting chile is in the air, and even today, when I go by Wagner's
Farm Store, I roll my windows down to smell the chile roasting. September is
the best time to campaign for a general election in these areas. It isn't too
cold and I always came home with the fragrant fresh picked chile, tomatoes,

✪ Corrales, July 4 parade, 1988.

corn, and in a good season, apricots from Placitas. A great connection is made with the people when you can sit down in their homes, sample their delicious harvest, and talk about the issues they are concerned about. In the town of Bernalillo, my friend Justin Rinaldi would take me to visit with the Sena family. They had vineyards, made delicious wine, and I always had to share a glass with the family. Justin's family used to have vineyards in Bernalillo and he still made wine also.

Ronnie Sisneros had family in Peña Blanca, and he took me to visit them when I was a candidate for Senate. Our dinner that evening had fresh corn, tomatoes, and chile. Dulcie Curtiss and her daughter, Evelyn Losack, good friends in Corrales, always sent me home with gifts of the garden. They are State Fair prize winners for their jams, jellies, and herbs, and they share these with me also. Burt DeLara's family in Placitas had old apricot trees, and I love stone fruit. I was the recipient of a couple of bags of apricots one year, as the fruit is fickle and it comes infrequently.

Campaigning is very hard work, with lots of preparation, gathering volunteers, raising money, planning coffees, rallies, and speeches.

I was the Sandoval County chairwoman for Toney Anaya's successful campaign for governor in 1983. At that time, I was the vice chairwoman of the county and Arnold Rael was the Democratic county chairman. However, Ruben Miera was still the patron of the county, and he was the acknowledged

⊕ Campaign rally in Algodones coordinated by Ruben Miera, Sandoval County Democratic Party chairman for Ray Powell for governor.

leader of the county for many years during the Montoya family leadership, when Joe Montoya became a U.S. Senator. I remember that Arnold and Ruben were supporting Aubrey Dunn for governor, and Arnold and I had a wager of a bottle of champagne, which he delivered to me, concerning the victor of the campaign.

The preprimary convention was difficult, but it was significant because it demonstrated the beginning of the change in Sandoval County, caused by the new community of Rio Rancho and its growing population. In those days, the Rio Rancho majorities were new residents from the eastern part of the United States and retired workers from the Midwest. There were a lot of Democrats. In New Mexico, as elsewhere, there are ethnic splits in voting patterns, and frequently Hispanics will support other Hispanics over Anglos, which covers everyone who is not Hispanic, even African Americans as James Lewis, the African American state treasurer, once told me. So we had Ruben Miera and Arnold Rael supporting the Anglo Aubrey Dunn and me and my Anglo Democrats from Rio Rancho, Corrales, and Placitas supporting Toney Anaya. But a lot of Hispanics from the rest of the county also wanted Toney Anaya, and of course he got the majority of the votes. It was one of the first times that the patron could not deliver the votes as he wished. In later years Ruben and I worked well together and supported the same candidates. A friend recently told me Ruben Miera had given me quite a compliment when he said, "Pauline kept her skirts clean."

It was after this, that many of my friends and political observers came and suggested that I run for office myself, rather than running other people's campaigns. We discussed it in the family and Mel said yes, I should make an effort if the right opportunity presented itself. Todd was already away studying at Brown University, and Keith was a sophomore at Cibola High School and he liked the idea of my running for office. They were all very supportive and walked and knocked on doors for me, and for many years the people in Rio Rancho would ask about my sons, because they liked it when the boys came to their doors and said, "Would you please vote for my mom for the legislature, as she is the best."

Maintaining the family, campaigning, and then fulfilling the job as a public official is not an easy task for women candidates, and it is necessary to have some help. My husband and son helped with the campaign but I was fortunate to have help in the house also. Ms. Elsie Janovek was hired to be home with the boys when I was working for Energy Consumers. She arrived at 3:00 p.m. and stayed until 6:00 p.m. for three days a week, as I was working part time. Elsie turned out to be a wonderful cook and she began preparing dinner three days a week and that was how I managed to do all the activities that I did during the years when our sons were still at home. All of us grew to love Elsie and her sister Artene Foxwell. We also had the help of Christine Romero one day a

○ Campaign picture with my guys, Todd, Keith, and Mel, at the Kiva ladder in Coronado Monument.

week for all of those years, and she is still helping us in the house, but now she is also a trusted friend of the family.

I have noticed that other women who hold public office have the same problems with maintaining the household while attending constant meetings and being responsible for the public's governmental business. This is a difficult problem for many families when both parents are working, and they find solutions through family help, hired help, and a lot of struggling, particularly when children are small.

House District 44, which I won in 1984, was all of Corrales, Bernalillo, and Rio Rancho as redistricted in a special election on September 18, 1984, for the primary and November 6 for the general election. We had been in Florida for my niece's wedding and returned home on August 20, to find that the court had redistricted, based on the 1980 census and the population shift to Rio Rancho. The census had always been incorrect with regard to the growing population in Rio Rancho, which is now the third largest city in New Mexico. In 1984 the census indicated that there were seventeen thousand people living in Rio Rancho, but there were already twenty-five thousand or more, and that lag of correct data continued. In later years, my House district included portions of Rio Rancho and my Senate District 9 went over the mountains to Cedar Crest and Sandia Park to the east of Albuquerque. I always had the fastest growing district in the state, with all of the infrastructure problems, crowded schools, and the need for more police and fire protection.

When the special election was announced, there were other people interested in the primary, however I think I had an edge because I had run in the 1983 primary and narrowly lost to the incumbent Ricky Kloeppel. The advantage I had was a campaign committee that had been established for that campaign, and they were willing to help in this effort, which came very quickly.

As I've looked back at my calendars from those years, I see that there was an explosion of activity on those months before campaign deadlines. The format I used for this first full campaign was to use separate committees in each of my communities, as they are so different. Corrales was still a small suburban village with about two thousand people; Bernalillo was an historic Hispanic town of four thousand people, and Rio Rancho a burgeoning city with twenty-five thousand people. The challenge is always to get your voters identified and to the polls to vote. The voter registration in Bernalillo was always very high because they usually had candidates running for sheriff, county clerk, county appraiser, county treasurer, and county commissioner, and there are a lots of large families in Bernalillo that help each other.

There were about a dozen large families that I visited with and got support from many, but I also walked in the new areas of the east side of the town of Bernalillo. Walking and knocking on doors requires that you recruit all of your friends and people that you have worked with or gone to school with, or my husband's law school friends, my tennis friends, or my son's friends and ask for a few hours on the weekends. One of my friends from the University of Florida, named Jennie Negin, walked all through parts of Bernalillo with me that September, and we laughed about this new experience together.

A number of people helped me in the town of Bernalillo, including the Rinaldi family of John and Susan, Justin and Maria, as well as Priscilla Abousleman and Orlando Lucero. They helped me with walking, particularly Justin Rinaldi, meeting people, putting up signs, and making suggestions about how to campaign in Bernalillo, where politics at that time was conducted family by family.

⊛ Wayne and Jolene Maes, longtime campaign coordinators for my
telephone campaigns.

Corrales has a one-house-per-acre requirement, so walking is not that
productive, except in certain areas like the business district. Coffees, house
parties, picnics, and calling on the phone were the most effective ways to reach
people. I had the good fortune of having a lot of friends who helped in that
first campaign and all of the other ten campaigns that I had while running for
office during my legislative career.

Jolene and Wayne Maes developed a phone committee with scripts for
the callers and tally sheets for the precincts that they called, so we were able
to identify our supporters. They were very serious about this and my part was
to gather up the volunteers to make the calls. It worked very well and we used
the same model in Rio Rancho and Bernalillo.

Frank and Juliet Marquez were also early and important volunteers. I met
Frank when he worked for Jack O'Leary in the Energy Department in Santa Fe.
They helped with parties, walking, calling, and overall strategy. Frank helped
me in Santa Fe one session, and he went on to work for Sandoval County and
now Bernalillo County. Viki and Clifford Pedroncelli were early supporters,

○ Viki Pedroncelli and Estevan, Tony, and Shauna visiting the capitol.

and they helped with calling and walking as well as Cliff's help with all of the old-timers in Corrales. He had served on the Village Council for many years. He was very young when his family moved to Corrales and Cliff knew all of the old families. We are still friends and their son Estevan has worked for me in Santa Fe when I was in the Senate. Estevan went on to follow in his dad's footsteps and became a village councilor and their other son, Tony, worked for Albuquerque mayor Marty Chávez as a top assistant.

Another early supporter was George Mannierre. He helped by holding a party at his home and introducing me to his daughter, Nora, and his son-in-law Victor Scherzinger, who had a printing business called Cottonwood Printing. Victor became a very important part of all of my campaigns, as he helped me with my brochures and also introduced me to Michael LaFlamme, who designed my brochures and literature. Victor not only helped me but many other candidates and many organizations in Corrales who needed printing.

I've already mentioned the help of Dulcie Curtiss and her family, Evelyn Losack and Dorothy Trafton, also Pete and Pat Smith and Tommie and Jim Findley. The village has grown and changed, but I will always remember all of the people who helped and supported me in the early campaign, and they continued to help through my whole career.

My husband was Corrales Municipal Judge from 1980 to 1990, and we always laughed about whether that was helpful or harmful to my campaigns. Our younger son would always ask him to go easy on his friends, who were in court for speeding, and Mel would tell him not to ask or he would have to recuse himself from the case. Mel's help was immeasurable, in the support I got at home and his encouragement for me to run for public office. His attitude was, if it is something you want to do, then you should try to achieve your goal. It never seemed to bother him that I was in the spotlight, probably because he had always had so much success in his multiple careers.

Campaigning in Rio Rancho was quite different than the other areas in my district because it was so large and the pivotal points of the community were less defined. How to reach the registered voters was the question we tried to answer as best we could. This was dependent on having enough volunteers to help with the phoning, walking, and speaking for me in the volunteer groups: Parent Teacher Association, Baseball League, Senior Center, Italian American Club, Jewish Community Center, Chamber of Commerce, Rio Rancho Rotary Club, Kiwanis Club, and the political leadership.

I met Marlene Feuer when she was on the Rio Rancho City Council and we became family friends. She and her husband Steve helped me by introducing me to their friends in Rio Rancho, and they became the core of my campaign volunteers during this first campaign. Bobby Droske, who has since moved away, organized the walkers with a group of friends, including Joan (now deceased) and Fred Kellogg, Glenda and Cal Mowry (now deceased), and Ann and Vic Heid. They all had children and I remember that after the *Albuquerque Journal* and *Albuquerque Tribune* endorsed me for the position of

⊙ Knocking on doors with volunteers, including Gail Horan, Marlene Feuer, Paul Turpen, and Jules Rubenstein.

EVERYONE ENDORSES

PAULINE EISENSTADT!

"No one does more for her people than Pauline Eisenstadt."

Senator Jeff Bingaman

"Her accomplishments are impressive."

Congressman Bill Richardson

"Pauline Eisenstadt has earned our respect with hard work and solid leadership."

Former Governor Bruce King

"Pauline was the person responsible for getting the Paseo del Norte Bridge Bill passed in the House. I know. I watched it all."

Rep. Dick Minzner
Chairman, House Taxation and Revenue

The *Albuquerque Journal* endorses Pauline Eisenstadt.

The *Albuquerque Tribune* endorses Pauline Eisenstadt.

The *Rio Rancho Observer* endorses Pauline Eisenstadt.

Paid for by the Committee
to Re-elect Pauline Eisenstadt.
Printed by Cottonwood Printing.

✪ Campaign cards, distributed just before the election, 1988.

state representative, we made copies of the endorsements and drove through the district with all the kids, and they put them at the doors of the voters.

I was helping to get the volunteers who did the walking, and we had precinct lists with addresses of the registered voters and maps of the streets in Rio Rancho. This requires a lot of organizing, and we walked on weekend mornings in teams of two people each. This pattern was established for all of my successive campaigns and it worked. I never lost a campaign after that first primary. In that campaign I lost to an incumbent in a district that did not include many precincts in Rio Rancho. In later years I had the continued support of all of the people who helped early in my career and added many more, such as Jules Rubenstein, who became the only person in Rio Rancho who could deliver large numbers of votes for a campaign. Jules would work every day, talking to people all over the community, and he became a favorite of many candidates. He later worked in the Sandoval county clerk's office. He died in a road accident around 1988 and we all miss him still. Jules was in his eighties when he was walking with me and knocking on doors looking for votes in my 1986 campaign. I got tired and wanted to quit, but Jules always said, "Let's just do one more block. They want to meet you, Pauline." He had this big smile on his face, and people liked him and trusted him, which is always the key in politics.

⚙ My favorite campaign sign. In front of old Price's Dairies on 528 in Rio Rancho. All the cows were supporting Pauline.

Irv Roth was one of the pioneers in Rio Rancho, as he came in the 1960s working with Amrep Southwest, which was the developer that created the community out of the desert. Irv Roth knows all about the community and its history, and we worked together on many issues for the community, particularly the Paseo del Norte Bridge and the need for a new school district. He came to Santa Fe to testify in the Appropriations and Finance Committee when I was working on legislation for the bridge. Irv helped by chairing my fundraising committee in my first campaign, and he helped in the successive campaigns as well. Lydia Horowitz helped with the phoning, and in those days she also helped with some walking. Paul Turpen moved from Portales to Rio Rancho and he helped by coordinating the walkers in a later campaign.

John and the late Aida Econopouly coordinated my Senate campaign walkers. John was one of our tennis player friends, and he had a delightful manner with everyone. We would meet at their house at nine-thirty in the morning, have bagels and coffee, get instructions and maps, and start knocking on doors. The plan was to meet at a restaurant, usually a pizza place, and bring in the maps and remaining brochures and exchange the funny stories that happened along the way on the campaign trail. I never walked alone in case there were some angry voters, but I never came across an angry voter. However, there were some unusual ones. Once, I rang the bell and after a short time a man came to the door and he was completely nude. I was quite

○ Party at Bill and Yvonne Joiner's place. John Econopouly, with the sunglasses, coordinated my walking with volunteers all over Rio Rancho.

surprised and not interested in having a conversation with him, so I left quickly and called to my partner, who was on the other side of the street, to share this happening. Most of the stories were about dogs, more people who wanted to volunteer, and issues they were concerned about for the legislature to address.

Walking and talking to people in the neighborhoods was the most effective way to find out what is happening in their communities, and what they are concerned about and want some help with from the elected officials. In statewide races, it is not possible, and other ways of reaching the target audience are used, like TV advertising, radio, and newspapers. Since my last campaign in 1996 for the state Senate, the methods of campaigning have changed dramatically because of new technology. The computer and Internet technology revolution have made it mandatory to use e-mails, websites, Facebook, and many other kinds of new technology. Also, fundraising on the Internet is relatively new. Nationally, Howard Dean, candidate for president, pioneered the use of the Internet for fundraising, and in this last cycle of campaigning President Obama raised enormous amounts of money on the Internet with many small contributors.

The methods have changed for reaching an audience with one's message. I had a cable TV message during my race for the Senate on the Rio Rancho cable

Bowling fundraiser in Rio Rancho. From left, Rudy Miller (deceased); Mel; Art Trujillo, State Democratic Party chairman; and Irv Roth.

Mayor Tom Swisstack and former wife Kathy.

Mayor Marty Chávez, left, and Albuquerque city councilor Sam Bregman, who was kneeling.

station, and it seemed to have a nice size audience. I still think that in local races, where possible, shaking someone's hand and talking to them makes a big difference. People running for office in Sandoval County often come to me for advice about winning an election, and I always suggest walking and talking to the voters. Daymon Ely came for advice in his race for Sandoval county commissioner, and I suggested walking until he wore out his tennis shoes. He won his race, and I got a package one day with a note of thanks and his worn

⊕ Roy and Norma Montoya with our granddaughters during holidays
at Santa Ana Pueblo.

out tennis shoes. Daymon went on to become a good and competent chairman of the county commission when a lot of decisions were made about our
future in the county.

My district included Santa Ana Pueblo, before the casinos, and in later
years my Senate district included Sandia Pueblo and the East Mountain communities of Sandia Park and Cedar Crest. I had many friends at the pueblos,
and I very much enjoyed visiting and talking about their concerns. Santa Ana
Pueblo is a favorite of mine, and we still visit with Roy and Norma Montoya
and their family during the Christmas holidays if we are in town and take our
children if they are visiting. We have attended their weddings, and they have
attended our children's engagement parties in Corrales. A memorable election
night conversation came from my campaign volunteer for Santa Ana Pueblo.
He called to tell me the results and he asked if I wanted the good news first or
the bad news and I said the good news. He said, "There were 100 votes, and
you got 97 and the other candidate got 3 votes. But don't worry, I know who
the other votes were and I'm going to get them." I wish I could do as well in
all the precincts.

With new communities in my district, I had to make new friends and
find out about the area and their concerns. In the East Mountains Jennifer and
Albert Noyer became friends and advisors for me about the area, as well Geri

Ostrow, editor of the *East Mountain Telegraph* newspaper, who also helped me understand the community. I remember attending the Mountain Man Rodeo, which was a big fundraiser for the community, held at the top of the ski area. I was invited to judge the chile contest with County Commissioner Les Houston. After tasting a spoonful of about twenty different kinds of chile, I had to stop on the way home and regurgitate even the best of them. I learned not to judge chile contests, or let people throw sponges at me, or put me in jail to raise money in the community. My job was to help set public policy on major issues in Santa Fe, and I decided there were a lot of others who could do those things.

There was one incident during my first campaign that I want to describe because it became a lesson for the future campaigns. My opponent in the general election was a Republican named Don Doench, and he had put out copies of the sample ballot with a circle around his name. The line that made that circle covered up my name on the ballot. This happened during the last few days of the campaign and people began to call me. They were upset and so was I. The election code did not permit this to happen on the sample ballot or any reproduction of it. So there we were on Monday morning before the election on Tuesday and trying to decide what to do about this situation. My husband, the lawyer, decided to request an immediate hearing with District Judge George Perez for an injunction, which is an order from the court prohibiting someone from doing something.

We went to court on Monday morning with two witnesses who had copies of the sample ballot with my name circled out and the judge ruled in our favor. People said, "So what difference will this make as the election was tomorrow," but I took the order and the sample ballot to the TV stations and the radio station, and they taped a segment with me describing what had happened. That evening on TV the headline was "Dirty Tricks in Sandoval County." My husband said the lesson I learned was to marry a lawyer. The lesson I took from this incident that has stayed with me for all of my future campaigns is that the last few days of a campaign are very crucial. I always had a final piece of literature designed and ready to go if I needed something in the final days to counter statements that were not true. I never had another incident on the final days, but campaign consultants always warn about this, because usually it is too late to respond when the dirty tricks go out to the public.

I won that campaign and have won every campaign I have entered since then, but I've never taken a campaign for granted. The public always wants to know what you have done for them lately, and they want to be asked for their support. My legislative record has been very active, and when I held office I attended meetings all year, read all the newspapers in my district, invited groups to visit in Santa Fe, had children come up to visit the capitol by the busload, invited pages to help in the Senate, returned phone calls, and tried to help solve problems in the district.

✪ "Getting campaign help" from Governor Bruce King and Alice King.

✪ Classroom visit, 1989.

The Senate campaign was different because it was the largest district in the state, as the growth of Rio Rancho and the other suburban areas was rapid. The portion of the East Mountains that I had in my district was small but also growing fast. There was a group called the East Mountain Legal Defense Fund that worked on land use issues, and they got in touch with me during the campaign. Some of their members were Josh Simms, Bert Snipes, Susan Clair, and Kathy McCoy, who later ran for the House of Representatives and won. They wanted to talk about zoning issues and particularly about a Wal-Mart Superstore that was planning to locate across the freeway from a middle school in Tijeras. I attended a few meetings with large crowds that were opposed to the location. I agreed that it seemed to be a bad location and told them I would ask the State Highway Department to investigate for traffic problems. They appreciated my willingness to try to help, as I was the first politician that had agreed to help them. Mayor Jim Baca of Albuquerque also spoke out about the location. In small communities, as I had learned in my earlier research, the big issues are often about roads, bridges, sewers, and zoning.

The campaign was larger than most New Mexico State Senate races, as I had about seventy-five thousand people in the district, compared to most Senate districts, which were supposed to be in the range of thirty-five thousand people. My campaign administrator for this race was Sam Thompson. Sam helped on issues, brochures, mailings, and press releases, and she was terrific, dependable, and good to work with during the campaign. She worked for me in Santa Fe during the session and continued to work in Santa Fe for Attorney General Patricia Madrid and Attorney General Gary King.

○ Pauline testifying in committee on a bill, with help from Alice King.

✪ Working the floor of the House with Representative Ben Luján, then whip and later Speaker.

✪ The Corrales Senior Center with Dulcie Salce Curtis and friends.

⚙ Meeting in Rio Rancho, Representative Bob Perls and district attorney, and former lieutenant governor, Mike Runnels.

The fundraising got easier as I became a known quantity and I received many endorsements from the groups represented in Santa Fe, such as teachers' groups, police groups, fireman unions, pueblos, professional groups of realtors, physicians, children's advocacy groups, accountants, dentists, the *Albuquerque Journal*, the *Albuquerque Tribune*, and many more. I did not have an opponent in the primary, but I put on a full campaign and walked all over the district as I always did in past campaigns. I was running against a Republican incumbent named Virgil Rhodes, who had a primary challenger named Duke Rodriguez.

Virgil beat his opponent but I got more votes, without an opponent, than they both did together. For anyone watching that race closely, it was clear that I had a good chance of unseating an incumbent and that is what happened. I was the only Democrat to unseat an incumbent Republican in the Senate that year. My legislative districts were swing districts, because the margin between the registered Democrats and the registered Republicans was small, and the independents and moderates in both parties decide the outcome. There are usually about 30 percent of party activists on both sides that will vote a straight ticket and most of the other voters will consider the candidates on their merits, as well as their party affiliations. In swing districts that are growing fast and changing a lot, the candidate that works harder has a better chance of winning because there are so many new people that don't have the history of the community with which to judge the candidates. Senate District 9 had gone to the Republican candidate and recently swung back to the Democratic candidate with the election of John Sapien. I always felt that after I won the election I represented everyone in the district, and I tried to be open to their points of view even if they had not voted for me. That seemed to work well during all of my years of service in the legislature. You can't forget who sent you but the job is always explaining why you voted the way you did on many issues.

I enjoyed campaigning when I visited with the people, but the effort is Herculean and consumes one's life during the campaign season. Once I found the luxury of only campaigning every four years in the Senate, it was much easier for me. A person has to want to serve in public office to continue to put themselves in these campaigns. Most of my colleagues didn't have races to run, because they were in safe districts and didn't have competition in the general elections. It seems that today the Democrats are having challengers in their primaries, and this demonstrates that everything is always changing in politics.

CHAPTER SIX

The New Mexico Legislature and the National Conference of State Legislatures

A mind that is stretched by a new experience can
never go back to its old dimensions.

—Oliver Wendell Holmes

My legislative career began in the House of Representatives in 1985. I served there for eight years, chairing the Majority Caucus for four years. I also chaired the Rules Committee and served on the Appropriations and Finance Committee; Education Committee; Judiciary Committee; Government and Urban Affairs Committee; Consumer and Public Affairs Committee; and the Enrolling and Engrossing Committee, a committee that never met. I guess it had a purpose in the past.

I didn't serve on all of these at the same time. It was most common to serve on a major committee that took up all of my time and then some less busy committees. The schedule of the committee was determined by the number of bills that were referred to be heard and voted on, or tabled and not scheduled to be heard. This latter method was used sometimes by the chairman of a committee to kill a bill without having a hearing. This is something I learned to watch carefully at the end of the session because then it was easy to run out of time to send a bill to the Senate and go through its process of committee hearings.

When I was caucus chairwoman that was one of the things that made our House members the angriest, the slow fashion the Senate had of hearing the House bills. One of my friends from Sandoval County once took off his cowboy boot and started to scream about the Senate Judiciary Committee that

⊕ National Conference of State Legislators.

had not scheduled his bill for a hearing and the session was almost over. He said, "I don't care if they kill it, but at least give me a hearing," and he banged his boot on the table to punctuate his anger. There is a natural tension built in between the House and the Senate that really builds up steam at the end of the session.

The Speaker of the House appoints members of the National Conference of State Legislatures (NCSL), and I attended my first meeting in 1986. The NCSL is the official representative of the country's 7,461 state lawmakers and their staffs. It is the only national legislative organization governed and funded directly by the states. NCSL was created in January 1975 from the merger of three organizations that served or represented state legislatures. It's a nonpartisan organization with three basic objectives:

to improve the quality and effectiveness of state legislatures;
foster interstate communication and cooperation; and
assure state legislatures a strong, cohesive voice in the federal system.

The full membership of the NCSL elects officers and ratifies conference policy at its annual meeting. The governing body of NCSL is a forty-eight member Executive Committee, composed of thirty-two legislators and sixteen professional staff members, who take office each year in December. I mention this in such detail because I was nominated to serve on the Executive Committee in 1987. It was very exciting, as Irv Stolberg, the Speaker of the Connecticut House,

✪ The Executive Committee of the National Conference of State Legislators;
I served on this committee as an elected member for three years.

asked if I would like to serve on the committee. I was pleased to say yes, but first
I had to get the endorsement of both the Speaker of the New Mexico House and
the president of our Senate. They also agreed. I think I benefited from the need
to have more women on the NCSL Executive Committee.

Most of the other members were leaders in their state legislatures, and
I learned a lot about how other states function and made a lot of friends. I
brought a lot of information back to New Mexico and helped start some initiatives in our state that I learned from other states. It also became apparent to
me that we have lots in common with all other legislatures: budget problems,
leadership battles, end-of-session crashes, partisan fights, and fundraising for
campaigns, just to name a few of the areas that we could discuss together.
My term was for three years, and it required that I attend quarterly meetings
including the annual meeting. When the meeting was in Hawaii, I decided
to skip it because I knew that would appear in the newspaper as a junket, for
sure. This was not a paid position; I got per diem from New Mexico and an
airline ticket to attend meetings, usually in Washington, DC. The per diem
was seventy-five dollars then and the hotels in Washington were considerably
more. I thought the value of the experience was worth the difference, so I covered it with my own funds.

One of the issues that I brought back home was the idea of a Futures Commission that I learned about from a colleague in Kentucky. They had developed a group from all over the state to look into the future and try to develop

⊙ Pauline and Senator George Mitchell, majority leader of the U.S. Senate.

⊙ Pauline and Senator Al Gore when he was planning to run
   for president for the first time.

a plan for their future and then try to move in that direction. By the time I was in my third session, it became apparent to me that we had a lot of issues that could not be solved in our districts, but needed to have statewide solutions. The person I began to discuss this idea with was Clay Buchanan, the director of the Legislative Council Service. He was described as the Roundhouse encyclopedia because of his knowledge of the legislative history and the people that had been involved since he started to work for the legislature in 1954. Clay kept a coffeepot hot and had a conference table in the back of the office that attracted legislators, lobbyists, and journalists. It was a great place to swap ideas, test a new idea that might solve a problem, and borrow from other states. I remember suggesting we try the gadget called a breathalyzer for our drunken driving problem, and everyone told me it would not work in New Mexico. I did not follow through on that idea, but now we do use them and I'm pleased to see the deaths from DWI going down in New Mexico.

It was at this coffee table in 1985 that I began to talk to Clay about the idea of a Futures project for New Mexico, and he recommended that I talk with former governor Jack Campbell. Governor Campbell had established a planning division in state government, which no longer existed, and I don't believe we have a state planning division today, twenty-five years later. The need continues for a planning division in state government. Alvin Toffler, author of *Future Shock*, wrote, "Our political decision-makers swing widely back and forth between doing nothing about a problem until it explodes into crisis and alternately, racing in with ill-equipped, poorly assessed crash programs."

Governor Campbell suggested we get in touch with Bob Hoffman, who had a statewide network in the business community. He liked the idea and was instrumental in bringing it forward. We put together a group representing different organizations in the state that included people such as Sky Jencks and Bing Grady of Sunwest Bank; Jim Wall of Amrep Southwest; myself; and Bob Hoffman of the Economic Forum. The following people served as volunteer staff during that first year of discussion: Nancy Magnuson of the University of New Mexico; Harold Morgan of Sunwest Bank; John Parker of the City of Albuquerque; John Daly, economic consultant; and Joel Jones of the University of New Mexico. We began to talk about what we wanted to achieve and how to do it.

We agreed that a broad-based statewide private sector initiative was necessary to have the necessary impact for New Mexico. We had a public meeting in June 1986 to discuss our Futures Project with invited leaders in the community and the state. The guiding questions were: where are we now in our state's economic development, where do we want to go in the future, and how do we want to get there?

I was doing research with the help of the National Conference of State Legislatures and found these other models: the Arizona Academy, which sponsored Arizona Town Halls; the Colorado Front Range Project; the Task Force on the Future of Illinois; Kentucky Tomorrow; North Carolina 2000; and twenty more states with some kind of futures project. Many were created to deal with state economic growth, though most dealt with the entire scope of issues affecting the states: transportation, health care, environment, water, education, housing, and agriculture.

Most Futures projects were experiments in anticipatory democracy consisting of two basic elements: anticipation of the future and citizen participation. A natural outgrowth of any future project is legislative foresight, which means the legislative process anticipates and deals with the approaching problems, issues, needs, and opportunities. The National Conference of State Legislatures describes five reasons for the need for a formal legislative capability: issues are becoming more complex, issues the states must deal with have a long time frame, the impacts of a decision may extend far into the future, many issues are easier to deal with in their earlier stages than later, and impacts of science and technology in policymaking are expected to grow.

The paragraph above was taken from a speech that I gave at our public meeting in 1985, and I'm struck by the need to accomplish the same tasks today. My final comments that day are still true today: that the best way to ensure our own well-being is to ensure the well-being of our children. We can do this by giving them the tools to participate in society, working to strengthen the New Mexico economy so that our children will be able to find meaningful jobs within our borders, preserving our quality of life, and acting financially responsible and politically courageous so that we are not burdening our children with our debts.

Edward Cornish of the World Future Society said, "The future does not just happen to us, we ourselves create it by what we do and what we fail to do." That was my final challenge to our Futures project group as there was another group also discussing these topics, and our U.S. senators Bingaman and Domenici wanted the two groups to merge. From this merger we became New Mexico First. I served on the first board of New Mexico First, but my legislative obligations kept me too busy to continue at that time. New Mexico First followed the town hall mode of Arizona and prepared and researched topics for discussions at town halls with participation all around the state. They still exist and make contributions to the body politic, and I'm pleased to recall my part in putting some of these ideas forward first at the coffee table in the Roundhouse with Clay Buchanan. I hope that a future governor would once again establish a state planning office for New Mexico.

Regarding the National Conference of State Legislatures, I must also state that two of my fellow Executive Committee members were indicted for corruption in their states of Texas and New York. One was the Speaker of the House in Texas. I knew him and liked him, and we worked on some issues

✪ Pauline and Senator Jeff Bingaman.

together. The other one was the president of the Senate in New York. Both are huge states with lots of opportunities for theft and corruption. As I found out later, the size of the state doesn't determine if there is corruption, but rather the honesty of the individual holding the public office.

In the Senate I served on the Finance Committee and the Conservation Committee, but during my legislative career I have served on more than sixteen interim committees. The memberships of the interim committees are selected by the Legislative Counsel Committee, with the members indicating their preference to the leaders. In the Senate I chaired the Committee on Higher Education and worked very hard to meet in different locations around the state and hear from the public and the university administrations and boards of regents of the various institutions.

At that time we had about twenty-five institutions of higher education for our small state, and one of the bills that Senator Billy McKibben and I cosponsored was to put a moratorium on building any new campuses or satellite learning centers for existing universities. We passed that bill, a Senate Joint Memorial.

The state of New Mexico pays for each student through a funding formula and for existing building maintenance, utilities, and insurance, but not for new buildings unless authorized by the legislature through the budget.

However, our bill only pertained to state funding, and some universities would use foundation money to achieve their goals of new buildings.

The other major goal I wanted to achieve was to develop a statewide board of Regents, as we needed to avoid duplication of curriculums and develop centers of excellence for each campus rather than trying to compete for students. The membership of this committee was always composed of senators and representatives from university districts, and they opposed this idea as they felt their influence would be diluted. This is an undertaking for a governor of the state, and I think that Governor Richardson may have started down this road by appointing a cabinet secretary for higher education. Two other committees that I served on during the interim in the Senate, the time between legislative sessions, were the Economic and Rural Development and Telecommunications Committee, and I was the vice chairman of the Information Technology Oversight Committee.

While I was in the Senate from 1997 to 2000 the world of technology was changing dramatically; the Internet was becoming more available, and laptops were provided for members of the Senate if they wanted them. I remember that I had to have my aide take it down to the floor every day and bring it back to my office after the floor session because I only had one computer for both the floor and my office. E-mails needed attention all the time. I was serving on the National Conference of State Committees regarding the rapid change in technology, and we discussed how it would affect the way politics functioned and how to respond to such rapid response of e-mail from all over the state. At that time we didn't know where the e-mails were coming from, and usually we wanted to respond to people in our district personally but not to everyone in the state.

That period was a time of great transition in the way we communicated with the people in our districts and also how campaigns came to embrace websites, e-mail, Facebook, and even Twitter. I always liked the new technology, and I introduced a lot of issues into the legislature regarding the new technology. But adapting to change is difficult for some, and they are slow to feel comfortable with how it impacts their lives. An example of this was Senate Bill 146, the Electronic Documents Act, which was an electronic signature bill, which authorized the use of an encryption for secrecy so that business could be conducted using e-mail for contracts with the state and all other potential uses that required privacy. I had some experts from Los Alamos Lab come to testify, and they passed around a sheet of paper with what looked like a Picasso painting drawn by a donkey, full of lines, circles, and meaningless drawings, and they said that is what their encryption looked like printed. The chairman of the Senate Judiciary Committee, Senator Michael Sanchez, pulled his pen out of his pocket and said, "This is the only way I will ever sign a contract." I suggested that would be fine, but there were other people in the state that wanted the option of doing it this new electronic way. The bill was passed with the chairman's vote and signed into law.

The debate about whether the new technological ways of accomplishing the same tasks is better than the old ways will continue for generations, but my time in the 1980s and 1990s in the legislature was an earthquake of new ways of doing things. Recently, I was invited to appear on *In Focus*, a show on the local Albuquerque Public Broadcasting TV channel 5, to discuss Governor Richardson's inaugural address of 2007. I wasn't able to go to Santa Fe, and Richardson's speech was not broadcast live as had been in the past, but I was able to watch it on channel 7, ABC, another of the local stations, which streamed it on the Internet. This was light years from what was available when I left Santa Fe in 2000.

The rules of procedure of the House and the Senate are different in some ways, and it affects how the leadership accumulates power. In the House the Speaker is all powerful. He or she appoints, with Legislative Council advice, committee chairs and members and determines which committee a bill is referred to and how many committee referrals it will have. The Senate has a different procedure, as the majority leader, with advice from the Committee on Committees, refers bills to a committee or committees and each senator can request which committee they want it referred to, to be heard and debated. This is a big difference, because the number of committees you have to go through is important as well as the makeup of the committees. When I arrived in the Senate and realized the difference, I was quite pleased. I felt it was a more egalitarian way to give all the members an opportunity to present their bills and have a better chance of getting them through the process. I well remembered introducing ethics legislation for a number of sessions and getting four committee referrals each time from Speaker Raymond Sanchez, who opposed my bill, even though it had three-quarters of the House members as cosponsors. The Speaker was following the old patron system of leadership in this situation, and I disagreed with this approach.

The president of the Senate was Manny Aragon, and he also had a great deal of power as he appointed the members of the Committee on Committees that appointed the membership to committees. Both Raymond and Manny held a great deal of power in their respective houses during my terms in the legislature, and they were both intelligent University of New Mexico Law School graduates who were aggressive and competitive with each other and with many of the legislators. In the House and the Senate I worked with Raymond Sanchez and Manny Aragon on many issues that they cared a lot about—First Amendment rights, civil rights, educational opportunity for all—and we worked for the welfare of the citizens of New Mexico.

⊙ Taking the oath of office.

⊙ Opening day at the legislature, my second term in the House, with Mel.

⊙ My mother Anne Bauman Cohen, my sister Mickey Greenspan, Representative Tom Atcitty, and Governor Bruce King.

Most of my time in the legislature was with these two legislators as the Speaker of the House and the president of the Senate. After experiencing this system for a while, I began to believe that a rotation of leadership would be more effective for all of us as the accumulation of power in the same hands was not productive over the long time. The sandhill cranes, which I've always watched flying near our home in Corrales, offer a metaphor about leadership. They fly in a V shape, with the leader in front, I asked my friend Jim Findley, a biologist, how the cranes picked their leader. He told me, "They rotate, because it is too hard on the leader to be in front too long." I've often thought the birds have something to teach us about leadership and the need for change.

Breaking Ground for the Bridge!

○ Breaking ground for the Paseo del Norte Bridge across the Rio Grande.

○ Bridge ground breaking.

The most important issue in my district during my first term in 1985 was the need for a new bridge across the Rio Grande to alleviate the agonizing trip for commuters from the westside communities, including Rio Rancho and Corrales, into Albuquerque, which lies mostly to the east of the river. Traffic stacked up for about an hour on the trip to work in the morning and on ride the home in the afternoon. The Speaker that year was Gene Samberson from

Lovington, and he held the position of Speaker with the support of a number of conservative Democrats and a coalition with all of the Republicans.

Representative Samberson was always fair with me, and I respected him although I had not voted for him as Speaker. He appointed me to the House Appropriation and Finance Committee, and it was a crash course for me in how the state general fund was constructed and how the state finances were used by the departments. This group of Democrats was not an easy group to maneuver during my first year in the House. The majority leader of the House was Representative Dick Minzner, and he presided over the majority of the Democrats that were not part of the ruling coalition. He had a tough job and he did it well. My task was to convince a majority of the seventy members of the House to help me reauthorize money from a severance tax bond and designate it for the Paseo del Norte Bridge, which ran through Representative Raymond Sanchez's district. Representing the wishes of his district, Sanchez opposed the bridge.

I began early in the session going to all the members on the floor and talking to them and explaining my problem and the need for the bridge. One of my friends told me later that whenever I talked to someone, Raymond came along and talked to the same person and expressed his opposition. So, my first encounter with the former and future Speaker was not exactly friendly. I had the votes of many Democrats as they understood the problem. The other members from the Westside enlisted the Republicans, and we got the bill passed to reauthorize the small amount for the bridge.

It is important to note that this issue had been at the forefront of a lot of people's concern for the future of the Westside, and I had a lot of people come to Santa Fe and testify in the Appropriations Committee on behalf of House Bill 51. Leading the charge for Rio Rancho was my friend Irv Roth, who had been working on this issue with the Rio Rancho Chamber, the business community, and numerous other groups for a couple of years. This bill had passed the Senate before but never passed in the House because it had been blocked. I have wondered if the leadership had been different that first year that I was in the House whether we would have been able to proceed with the bridge as quickly as we did.

Governor Toney Anaya was supportive, and I spent many hours in his office talking with his chief of staff, Danny Weaks, trying to figure out how to raise the remaining $43 million to pay for the right of way acquisition for the bridge. Finally the director of transportation, Larry Larrañaga (who later became a member of the House), brought up the idea of selling Debenture Bonds, which our state had not done before. That was the way we proceeded to procure the money for the bridge. Governor Anaya held a press conference at the Alameda Shopping Center in Albuquerque on the Westside, and he invited me to join him on the helicopter flight from Santa Fe. At the last minute he

✪ Pauline—acting speaker in the House of Representatives.

asked if we should include Representative Hal Stratton, and I said, "Yes, he helped with the Republican votes," so he joined us for the press conference announcing that the Paseo del Norte Bridge was going to be a reality. We later had a ground breaking ceremony and finally, in 1987, we had a celebration and opening of the bridge. I brought champagne to the event and we celebrated for about twenty-three years, because there is a need for another river crossing as I write this account of how hard it was to get the last one. My sons call the bridge the Pauline Eisenstadt Memorial Bridge as it was the topic of so many dinner conversations in our house. They knew it was a key issue for me in our area with our neighbors, friends, and constituents. It is interesting that the bridge is not located in my district but it impacted all of us on the west side of the river. It is another example of how so many issues are regional or statewide issues.

The Finance committees of both the House and the Senate control the flow of all of the bills that have an appropriation attached to them because the amount of available general fund money is not known until the budget is drafted, at which time the remaining funds become available for legislative bills. That means that all bills are presented in committee and tabled until the process gets to the end of the session and the General Fund Appropriation Bill is voted on in both houses. The House does the heavy lifting on developing the Appropriation Bill, although Senator Manny Aragon had the Senate Finance Committee drafting our own bill one year when I was on the committee. I chaired the subcommittee that heard the presentations of all of the smaller state agencies and voted on their requests. I was very fortunate in the beginning of my career to have a friend named Kay Marr, who had worked in state government and held the position of cabinet secretary for the Department of Finance Administration during Bruce King's last administration. She became my financial guru and mentor in helping me understand how the budget was crafted, what role the legislators played, and how to identify where the problems might occur and what the solutions might be for the state budget.

The governor's staff prepares a budget and the Legislative Finance Committee prepares a budget. Then the committees in the House and the Senate listen to the presentations, read the material, and try to make decisions that will be the best for the state. The state constitution requires that we must stay within our budget and not spend money that we have not collected through state revenue. The money for the state revenue comes from the severance tax permanent funds; the state investment permanent fund; the State Land Office permanent fund, which is set aside for education; income taxes from individuals and businesses; and a percentage of the gross receipts tax.

The major purpose of politics is the allocation of resources, or the budget for the state. The money is spent for education, healthcare, environment, economic development, child welfare, public safety, courts, judges, prisons, and all of the other government departments. When there is not a sufficient amount of money to meet the needs of the state, then taxes need to be raised, and legislators are reluctant to do this unless convinced that the need is justified. The state budget when I began in 1985 was just about $1 billion, and in 2010 it reached $5.4 billion. In twenty-four years there has been a lot of growth in our state. The population has grown, the needs have increased, oil and gas revenues have risen, and the state investments were in the $12 billion range before the recent downturn in the market. Legislators in future sessions will have some difficult decisions to make because the revenue is about $350–400 million below the appropriations level. As an energy state, we have always experienced the "boom and bust" effect of the price of oil and gas; the new ingredient is the escalation of money in the investment funds and their recent downturn. These same problems happened in the rest of the country, and I'm hoping that as the economy recovers, our state will be in better shape for the future.

In the House, when I served on the Appropriations Committee, the word went out to the committee members, verbally, that there would be "mark up" tonight. I asked what that meant, and I was told that we would decide late in the evening what bills would be passed. One of my friends on the committee said, "Don't eat or drink anything after five in the afternoon, because if you leave the meeting and go to the bathroom you might lose your bill." So that was when I learned that at certain junctures in the legislative process the one with the largest bladder wins. I had a couple of things I wanted in the budget

⊗ My visitors for the day from Corrales Elementary School.

⊗ Rio Rancho Senior Center guests visiting the capitol.

that year and one of them was a larger increase for university faculty salaries. I think I got it, but statewide salary increases require a lot of money, and the amount I got was only about $10 million for the whole state. I really learned how much I didn't understand that first year about the financing of the state.

There is a story that looms large in my memory that was instructive for me in many ways. I was in my second term in the House, and I was chairwoman of the House Rules and Order of Business Committee. During the thirty-day session the House Rules Committee determines if the Senate bills are germane and can be debated in committees. They must have a budget implication or an appropriation or be on the governor's call list to be germane for the Rules Committee. One of the leaders came to me and asked about a senator's bill, and I told him it was germane. He asked how did I know, and I told him I had read the bill. There was a pause, and he replied that he didn't want it to be germane. I said that he would have to find someone else to do that. He paused again and said, "Pauline, you have bigger *cojones* than anyone up here." I told him that I would take that as a compliment and walked away. But the message to me was that truth can be manipulated by power, as it is in the larger community everywhere. As a group of elected officials I felt that we needed to hold that bar a little bit higher for truth.

The senator's bill was insubstantial, and the point of the effort was to deny its passage to demonstrate the power of the leader over the process. This was an example of intimidation and the patron system wrapped in one issue that was hard for me to cope with during my career. I always had allies and other legislators that would help me, and I always tried to reform the system and improve it for the future. I was willing to take on some battles, and the media helped as the public also needed to be informed. The majority of my colleagues were always trying to do what they thought to be the right thing for the public welfare, but there were some who wanted to cultivate their own power, and they were not interested in building a consensus on issues or compromising. As a woman, it was more difficult, as I knew that I had to be willing to confront some of these guys when I didn't agree with them. I had to marshal my evidence and convince them. Over time I believe they respected my judgment, my willingness to cooperate with them, my hard work, and my concern for the welfare of the citizens of our state.

After serving in both the House and the Senate, I came to prefer the Senate. The Senate with its forty-two members is smaller and easier to deal with than the House with its seventy state representatives. Because of the Senate's smaller size, each senator has more influence. Also, serving in the Senate requires campaigning every four years as compared to every two years in the House. My districts were always fast growing and swing districts so campaigning was a big effort as compared to districts that were not changing as much.

CHAPTER SEVEN

Legislative Issues and Decision Making

People make history, and not the other way around.
In periods where there is no leadership, society stands still.
Progress occurs when courageous, skillful leaders seize
the opportunity to change things for the better.

—Harry S. Truman

M y first session on the floor of the House of Representatives found me seated between Representative Max Coll from Santa Fe on my left and Representative Bob Light from Carlsbad on my right. They were both veterans of the legislative process with Max Coll having already served eight terms while Bob Light was in his second term. They both became friends, and I learned a lot from each of them. Max had just reinvented himself as a Democrat; he had switched parties the previous session and was the final winning vote for the first term of Raymond Sanchez as Speaker. Max was on uneven ground with the Republicans, and the Democrats weren't sure about him either, but I was new and eager to learn how the system worked, and he was very kind to me and tutored me on the rules and the politics of the House.

During that first session, Max explained how to get along with my colleagues. I had a bill on final passage and someone had promised me his vote but voted against it. I was angry that he did not keep his word and wanted to give him a piece of my mind. Max said, "Don't do it. He'll just think that he was right to behave that way and besides, when your next bill comes up, he'll give you his vote out of guilt. Remember," he smiled, "we all have long memories here and you'll get your chance later." I think Max was one of the longest serving members of the legislature, devoting more than thirty years to public service. He knew the rules and understood the appropriation process extremely well.

He also cared about a lot of important issues and was instrumental in moving them forward for the welfare of the state. Max was very interested in providing funds for the Office of Cultural Affairs for Art in Public Places. He introduced a bill that I cosponsored, but it did not pass through the Appropriations Committee because of all the competing needs in the state. The following year we determined a new strategy that was called Art in Public Places, and it passed because it did not require an appropriation. Instead it directed that 1 percent of any new state building's budget be set aside for art, without specifying or restricting what kind of art. This would not have passed without the help of Tisa Gabriel of the Department of Cultural Affairs. She lobbied many of the legislators, and they realized that the money was not coming out of the general fund but from the cost of future building projects. The impact of this legislation was remarkable when the Roundhouse remodeling project was begun in 1991 and the cost of the project was about $32 million, as I recall. Our capitol is one of the most beautiful in the entire country because of the sculptures, paintings, weavings, and beauty everywhere. I have had other legislators comment to me about the beauty of art in our capitol, and I've told them how it was achieved. They are all envious of New Mexico. During my time in Santa Fe, two of the largest contributors of our gross receipts taxes were tourism and our art market, which was third after New York and San Francisco. I am always pleased to think that I played a small part in the beauty represented in our public places and particularly the capital city of Santa Fe.

In those early years I laughed a lot with Max as he had a lot of free time. If you looked under his desk on the floor of the House, you would usually find a stack of amendments to a number of bills that were not his bills. This was his way of confusing sponsors and killing a bill that he didn't think should pass on the floor. I learned from Max about the numerous ways to delay and kill a bill and also how best to fast track a bill, but controversial bills always require a lot of debate, and there is no way to fast track them. Passing legislation is like a rabbit getting through a pack of coyotes; if it comes out alive, it will usually have a smaller tail, one leg, and perhaps one ear left, but usually it will not survive. The number of bills introduced was usually over 1,500 in each house, and the normal number that became law was in the 350–400 range, so the percentage is very small and that is probably the way it should be in the legislature.

Representative Bob Light and I served on the Appropriations Committee together during my first term, and we learned to respect and like each other, although we did not often vote the same way on the issues. Bob would often say, "Let's go have lunch," and we would go and he'd have forgotten his wallet. So I bought lunch, knowing that Bob was probably one of the wealthiest people in the legislature. When the new department of Children, Youth, and Families was created at the urging of Alice King and a large group of advocates,

⊕ Reelection help from my friends. Left to right: Representative Dick Minzner, Judge Joseph F. Baca, Representative Toby Michael, Pauline, Representative Max Coll, and Mel Eisenstadt, 1989.

Representative Bob Light donated a large sum of his money in memory of his wife Johanna and to honor Alice King, who he admired a great deal. I don't recall another time when this happened, and it demonstrates Bob's generosity of heart and willingness to help in the large issues. Bob always liked to attend the National Conference of State Legislatures meetings, and since I was on the Executive Committee, I always tried to attend. Sometimes he would attend an Executive Committee meeting with me, and we always had great discussions about the issues because we had different points of view. I talked with Bob recently and told him about my memoir and he said, "I always tell people that I never met a more honest person than Pauline, but I didn't always agree with her on the issues."

My two seatmates were wonderful, and we continued to share the same seats for six years. At a certain point, they both began using ear phones to hear better, and it became harder for me to talk to them on the floor. I felt lucky to know both of them for so many years as they were intelligent, honest, hardworking public servants to be proud of, and they served New Mexico well during their time in the legislature.

I usually cosponsored a lot of bills, but was careful about not carrying too many bills as the main sponsor. Because my bills often broke new ground, they required a lot of work and committee hearings in both the House and the

Senate. Legislation doesn't always pass the first time, but if the ideas are followed up and introduced again they sometimes have a better chance of getting through to become a reality. The governors changed during my tenure, and depending on their philosophies of government, my legislation could reach the governor's office and then receive the veto. Governor Gary Johnson did not believe in passing anything that had an appropriation for new programs, so some of my ideas for new technology programs or the Institute for Public Service that I spent a lot of time developing got the axe with his veto pen.

Capital projects for all of my communities were bills that brought roads, bridges, sewers, water systems, community centers, fire trucks, ambulances, libraries, and additions to senior centers or new community centers. I always worked happily with Republicans and Democrats to help with these projects, and over the years I was able to help with many of these issues, such as the Paseo del Norte Bridge; soccer fields for Rio Rancho, Corrales, and Santa Ana Pueblo; Petroglyph National Park ($2.5 million); and $1 million for Unser Boulevard. Three of those mentioned above were statewide projects. Representative Gary Hocevar and I represented the Westside, and we were approached by a group called Friends of the Petroglyphs to help make the state contribution, as they had gotten commitments from our U.S. senators and our congressmen. The capital outlay comes from the severance tax fund and the government bond fund. At that time it was divided into three equal portions between the House, the Senate, and the governor. We were responsible for the House share of $2.5 million for the creation of the Petroglyph National Park, and that was a hard sell because it left a lot less money for the rest of the individual member's projects back home. I heard comments from the members that indicated they didn't think saving a bunch of rocks was worth that much money, and besides, nobody really knew what the message on the rocks was telling us. We worked hard and got help from the pueblo community and passed it as one of the House capital projects in 1988.

By this time I had been elected caucus chairwoman and Representative Toby Michael was majority leader. I went to him for help on this bill because he also served on the Taxation and Revenue Subcommittee that made the recommendations for the House bill. Toby was very helpful on this issue and a number of others, and I enjoyed working with him, as he had a good sense of humor and was a lively man with a big family and a big heart. The bill he helped me with on the floor of the House was called the Mammogram Insurance Coverage Bill, and my own radiologist, Dr. Michael Linver, had asked me for help on this issue. At that time, the insurance companies would not pay for a mammogram until a woman was forty years of age, but the guidelines for women at risk for breast cancer said they should have them earlier. My mother had breast cancer and my sister-in-law died from it, so I knew a little about breast cancer. In particular I knew that I was at risk because of my family history. Women like my friend, Joanne Huff, came from all over the state to testify about their own experiences with breast cancer. With tears in their eyes they told their own stories and asked that other women have the opportunity to have these mammograms earlier so they might be spared the late stage disease, when the cures were not so easy.

We went before the first committee and got a do pass, which allowed the bill to proceed to the Business and Industry Committee. We testified again, with the women willing to discuss the most delicate problems they had with breast cancer and the need to detect the problem as early as possible for the women at risk. The committee had a few members who sold insurance, and they sympathized but said that they were against mandated coverage from the legislature as it was not good policy; they voted no on the bill. I found out later that day that some of the committee members had breakfast with the insurance lobby, and they had the votes to kill the bill in committee. The identical bill had been introduced in the Senate as well as the House, so if I could turn the committee report around on the floor vote, I could then substitute the Senate bill for the House bill and still get it passed before our time ran out at the end of the session.

Toby Michael, the majority leader, was managing the floor and determining which committees would be reporting their bills out for discussion, and I explained what had happened in the committee on the mammogram bill. Toby understood breast cancer as he'd had someone in his family with the disease, and he agreed to help by speaking for not accepting the committee's report and opening it up on the floor for discussion. It was quite an emotional discussion as most of the women spoke for passage and many of the men as well, as they also had loved ones with breast cancer. The vote was close, but we passed the bill on the floor of the House, and I made the switch to the identical Senate bill so that the insurance companies could not deny paying for a woman to have a mammogram if they were at risk at an earlier age. Some issues remain clear in my mind twenty-five years later, and this was certainly one of those. I hope that it helped a lot of New Mexican women.

There are many different ways to get legislation initiated, they include bills, resolutions for constitutional changes, joint memorials for both houses to consider, and memorials for one house to consider. I learned to use all of these methods for introducing legislation. As I look back, the method that surprised me was the memorial because I used it to put forward some new ideas that became important programs later. The memorial does not have the force of law. It is a recommendation from the legislature, and it sometimes gets the ball rolling in a department to take some action, such as establishing a Prenatal Task Force. Many of these memorials as well as bills were discussed and vetted during the interim time between sessions when a lot of legislative work gets done by the interim committees. Among the memorials that were passed and later grew into legislation were the Petroglyph National Park Preservation Memorial; a joint memorial that marked the beginning of the Hispanic Cultural Center in 1986; Children and Families Memorial in 1986; Prenatal Task Force Memorial in 1986; Continuum of Services for Children and Families Memorial, which was introduced and passed three times as it was evolving; Women's Museum Exhibit Memorial; Nurse Midwifery Graduate Training Memorial; and Children's Rights Memorial.

The Nurse Midwifery Graduate Training Program was brought to my attention by Dean Estelle Rosenblum of the College of Nursing at the University of New Mexico in 1991. She told me about a program in another state with a large rural population that had a horse riding nurse midwife who delivered most of the babies in that state. The rural areas do not have a lot of pediatricians or obstetricians to deliver babies, and she thought that we should start training nurse midwives in New Mexico. The College of Nursing had applied for a federal grant, and they needed our state support. We passed the memorial, and the university established the program. The grant was for five years and they delivered 30 percent of the babies in the state of New Mexico.

However, eventually the five years ran out, and by that time I was in the Senate serving on the Senate Finance Committee. It was the end of a long day, I had a friend join me, and we were going out for dinner in Santa Fe after the Senate Finance Committee had finished its business. I went to my office about six-thirty in the evening, and there was a woman sitting there. All of my staff had left for the day, my friend was with me, and we were preparing to go out. I asked the woman if she could come back tomorrow and she started to cry. She said she had been there all day and couldn't get anyone to help her. People told her that I was the only one who could help her. I told my friend to go to the restaurant and I would meet her there, and I listened to the woman, who turned out to be the chairwoman of the Nurse Midwifery Program at the University of New Mexico. We needed to put this program in the budget for the University of New Mexico, College of Nursing, as it was a special program which had been funded by the federal government. Between the work I did with the Senate Finance Committee and that done by Representative Danice Picraux in the House Appropriations Committee, we were able to continue this program for our state's rural population. The program continues today and the College of Nursing honored me with a "Legacy to Nursing Award for Her Commitment to the Advancement of Nursing Education in 2002." This effort began with a memorial in 1991. A smart and caring dean, Estelle Rosenblum, of the College of Nursing and her staff developed the curriculum enabling a lot of wonderful trained nurse midwives to deliver babies in rural New Mexico ever since.

Other memorials that blossomed into something great for the state of New Mexico were the Children's Continuum of Care in 1988; the Children and Families Memorial in 1988; and the Continuum of Services, Children, and Families in 1990. The advocates for children's issues were wonderful and very effective as lobbyists for their cause. I remember seeing Corrine Wolfe and Joe Paul, who chaired the advocacy network, in the capitol every day as unpaid lobbyists during the sessions of the legislature. During the remodeling of the capitol, we were in the Public Employee Administration building across from the capitol and Corrine came in my office and asked where she could hang her coat. Of course, I said right here. So, I was lucky to start my day with Corrine Wolfe as she was one of the most dedicated people in Santa Fe for the welfare of children and families.

I worked closely with the child advocate group because I know that a child's early years would determine their adult lives, and it always was apparent to me that we needed to put the money in education and prevention of problems or we would pay more in prisons or mental health care later. The group of people that I worked with included Jolene Maes, my friend in Corrales; Angie Vachio, who founded Peanut Butter and Jelly, a preschool for mothers and children; Dave Schmidt, who worked in juvenile crime prevention and the juvenile code of laws; and many more dedicated people.

Governor Bruce King was elected for his third term in 1990 and that meant that we had the benefit of Alice King also, and she was the center of concern for the issues related to child welfare and families in the state of New Mexico. She provided a focus for the Continuum of Care advocates, and in 1991 the governor signed the bill that created the Department of Children, Youth, and Families. The advocates had been working for years to achieve this kind of focus on these issues and they finally achieved their goal. The memorials over three years had educated our legislators about the issues and the problems, and it gave me a lot of pleasure to vote for the department after all of the effort we had put into our concerns. I think we were the first state to establish such a department, and a great deal of the credit goes to Alice and Bruce King for recognizing the need to bring all of these issues together in a continuum of care and consolidating the departments to achieve these goals.

The memorial for the Women's Museum Exhibit focused on the roles women have played in the history of our state. I invited Representative Tweeti Blancett, a Republican from Aztec, to cosponsor this with me, and we got all of the eleven women in the House to cosponsor this also. Two years later I had a letter from Thomas Livesay, director of the Museum of New Mexico. He said,

> In your maiden bill in the New Mexico legislature, you charged the Museum of New Mexico with the task of developing a special curriculum devoted to the roles women have played in the history of our state. Approaching this challenge, we decided to develop a special issue of our magazine, El Palacio, since it is the Museum of New

Mexico's most far reaching program. We have subscribers throughout the fifty states, and a strong readership abroad as well. In addition, a printed piece, unlike an exhibition, will survive and be used
for years to come in the many libraries that receive the magazine. . . .
This has been an extraordinary project for the Museum. Newsstand
sales have been brisk, a clear increase in subscriptions has resulted,
and many compliments have been received from the general readership and scholars alike.

I was pleased to receive my copy and an offer of more complimentary copies from Director Livesay. The *El Palacio* issue was volume 92, number 10 of
the summer/fall 1986, edited by Malinda Elliott. I enjoyed reading the articles
and would hope that they do another one soon to capture the changing role of
women in our state. I'd like to quote from one article written by Joan Jensen who
was head of the Department of History at the New Mexico State University. She
edited a book with Darlis A. Miller called *New Mexico Women: Intercultural Per-
spectives*, published by the University of New Mexico Press in 1986: "Real political power was held by the political parties during the years after the 1920 vote
for the women's suffrage and women never had more than token power in the
political parties." A letter she quoted from Jennie M. Kirby, state vice chairman
of the Democratic Party in 1936, to Senator Dennis Chavez described Kirby's
frustration with gender politics.

I am tired and disillusioned. For fifteen years, regardless of all the
rebuffs received at the hands of many of the leaders of the party, I have
answered the call to service and have given of my time and strength to
interest the women in the Democratic Party and hold them. Instead
of receiving co-operation from the men in most instances I have met
with indifference and in many instances rudeness which few women
would have stood for. In 1920 at the National Convention, I heard the
cordial invitation extended to the women of the nation to come into
the Democratic Party and the most generous offer of a 50–50 repre-
sentation in the organization. Today I am wondering if it was just
a lovely gesture with little or no sincerity back of it. I have reached
the conclusion that the Democrats have no better understanding of
women in politics than their Republican brothers.

The role of women in politics has changed dramatically since 1920, but we still
only have thirty-four members of the legislature in the House and the Senate,
or 30 percent. When I started in 1985, we had thirteen women in the legislature, or 11 percent, so we are moving in the right direction, and I'm looking
forward to the time when we will have 50 percent of our female population
represented in our legislative body.

In the 2010 election New Mexico had two female candidates running for governor, Diane Denish, a Democrat, and Susana Martinez, a Republican. I think Denish had a wonderful opportunity to be the first woman governor, however Martinez was elected and became New Mexico's first elected female governor and the first Latina governor in the United States. She has my congratulations for her landmark achievement and my hope that she will accomplish a lot for the people of New Mexico.

CHAPTER EIGHT

Legislative Diplomacy
Trips to China and Japan

Travel is fatal to prejudice, bigotry and narrow-mindedness,
and many of our people need it sorely on these accounts.
Broad, wholesome, charitable views of men and things
cannot be acquired by vegetating in one little corner
of the earth all one's lifetime.

—Mark Twain

Lieutenant Governor Mike Runnels invited my husband and me to join him on a trip to China, sponsored by the Chinese People's Friendship Association. It was the spring of 1985, after my first session in the House of Representatives. I had worked with Mike on one of his projects that came before the House Appropriations Committee while I was a member of that committee. He initiated the MainStreet program for New Mexico and coordinated it from his office. The program's purpose is to help communities with historic preservation and economic development throughout New Mexico. The town of Bernalillo was one of the first small communities to take advantage of this program, and I believe the wine festival they hold yearly is an outgrowth of this program, through the efforts of its first director Maria Rinaldi. Corrales now has a very active MainStreet program that has been in place for a number of years, doing preservation work and economic development. I enjoyed working with Mike Runnels. He had a long history in New Mexico—his father had been a congressman and he had been a Santa Fe councilor. I thought he was innovative, involved in trying new ideas.

The arrangements for the trip to China required that my husband and I pay our transportation and the Chinese People's Friendship Association would host us in China. In 1985 memories of the Cultural Revolution were fresh (it had ended only seven years earlier), and China was opening up to the world. We were treated to great hospitality from the moment we arrived at the Beijing airport, and we were quite a sight for the Chinese. We were among the first Americans that many of the Chinese people had ever seen in person. Our group was small. There were five of us, my husband and me, Mike Runnels, and Senator Tom Rutherford and his wife Linda Rutherford.

The trip was a mix of meeting with officials and our hosts treating us to the tourist attractions, such as the Great Wall of China, the Ming Tombs, and the Forbidden City. The Chinese were always following protocol with our official visit, and since the highest official in our group was the lieutenant governor, we always met with a vice president or someone of that level of authority.

We met with the vice president of the Chinese People's Republic in the Great Hall of the People and had tea served while we sat on chairs that were so big that five people my size could have sat in one. The discussion went from Chinese to English, back to Chinese through interpreters and it could make you dizzy, but we were officials on an information gathering trip. In 2010, trips to China have specific business, such as trade deals to arrange, as the world has changed dramatically in the past twenty-five years. Our group was on Chinese television that evening, and I remember Mike taking pictures of the television news that night. We were featured in the newspaper as visiting dignitaries and had more drivers and interpreters with us than our five people. We were surprised by the attention we received for our small state of New Mexico and finally realized that as they were just opening to the world, we were symbols for the people. Historically, the Chinese always viewed themselves and their emperor as the center of the world and people came to pay tribute. We were the Americans coming to China. I had a class in Chinese history years ago, and that was something I shared and we talked about as we went from one reception to another.

Since I was female, we usually had one female in the meetings, particularly for dinner, or the banquets as they were called. One evening I sat next to a lovely lady who told me she was the mayor of a small town nearby. I inquired how many people in her small town and she said 10 million people, and I wondered if they knew that New Mexico had less than 2 million in the whole state. But, we were Americans, from the most powerful country in the world, and we had come to China. We were symbols.

The trip was planned along the eastern part of China. From Beijing we flew to Shanghai and spent about five days there with a guide and they housed us in a part of the old French Concession territory. In the late nineteenth century and in the brief period between the end of the Second World War and the victory of the communist revolution in 1949, European countries had settlements in Shanghai that were divided into concessions called the French, English, and American settlements. In Peking (now Beijing), where there were only one or two other hotels at that time, we had stayed at the Peking Hotel, but in Shanghai we stayed in a beautiful old house in the French Quarter, or Concession. Our guide was a fluent English speaker, and she informed us about what happened to her family during the Cultural Revolution. Both of her parents were educated in the West, and they were doctors from wealthy families. They were sent to the country to work on the farms with the pigs and the animals for about fifteen years. They were back in the city now, but she said they were broken people and never recovered from their deprivations during that time of their lives. Mao Tse Tung and Joseph Stalin had the same idea about the need to reeducate or kill the ruling class to conform to the new system of Communist rule. It seemed to me to be a foolish thing to stamp out many of your brightest and educated people. It would take generations to gain back their knowledge and leadership. Our guide confirmed this for me in Shanghai, but what we witnessed was an awakening in front of our eyes.

We arrived in Beijing to a sea of blue and grey Mao jackets, very few automobiles, and so many bicycles that you could hardly walk on the streets. Also, free enterprise was beginning and most bicycles became little stands selling cabbage or other foodstuff. In the countryside the patches of dirt by the roadside were all planted with vegetables, which were then taken to the city to sell, as the people were allowed to keep the money from their own garden plots.

The communist experiment was changing and allowing elements of capitalism to emerge all over the country. We were driven all over and visited communal farms using biomass from the cow manure to fuel cookstoves. They were using appropriate technology for everything as they had very little, except they had lots of people to take care of and their historic past indicated one famine after another.

I found their public policy of one child per family to be an interesting solution to the problem of overpopulation. How were they able to control that policy? We visited a farm, and they served us tea with a family of three generations; the grandparents, one son and his wife, and their only son of two years old. They all lived together and the little boy went from one lap to another. I thought he was well loved but was probably going to be a spoiled adult. I'm wondering if the present generations of "only" children are having trouble governing themselves. Recently at a lecture I heard these only sons referred to as "little emperors" who had indeed been very spoiled. The "little emperors" have not become leaders yet, and there is concern about how well they will work with others in a world economy.

In Shanghai we also spent a few days in a hotel on the Bund near the river and I decided to take a walk by myself. The walk attracted people. They were friendly but there were so many following me that I got scared. I think there were about a hundred people when I stopped. They wanted to touch me, and one talked to me in English, telling me he worked in New York years ago. My husband thought that my blue eyes and auburn hair was so unusual for them that they wanted to see me up close, but that was the last time I left the group.

One of the lasting impressions I have of China is the large number of people everywhere. Some of the art is very small, paintings on sea pearls, small clay figures, small necklaces. I think there is a connection with the art and the size of the population. The most beautiful ballet I have ever seen was a traditional Chinese ballet with violins, scarves of every size and color, and beautiful dancers. The children are trained as youngsters and they are enchanting in their execution of ballet.

We went to Guangzhou (formerly Canton), and there was more color in their dress, some blouses with flowers and shirts other than Mao jackets. There was a huge trade exposition selling many of the Chinese products wholesale. We saw some Europeans, Americans, Asians, and people from all over the world. This area was perhaps the center of the entrepreneurial activity.

We feasted at banquets every evening during our trip, and the one thing I didn't like was how the food was served to honored guests. An official on my right would select choice pieces of meat or vegetable from the lazy Susan tray with his chopsticks and then put it on my tray. He would then use his chopsticks as his eating utensils and then he would serve me again with his same chopsticks. Only occasionally would there be a separate pair of serving chopsticks. I never found a graceful way of objecting to this procedure, but we never got sick either.

We started out asking about the food and what it was, what part of the goose, chicken, or pig it was from, and finally we didn't want to know as they eat everything from all the parts of everything that walks, flies, or swims. One night we went to a restaurant, and there was a monkey jumping around in an atrium and it was gone when we left. We all suspected we had eaten it. It tasted good, and we really didn't know or ask what was on the platter.

We went to an economic zone near Hong Kong at the end of our two weeks in China, and we could see the planning and the effort they were making to develop new industry in these areas. We thought that some of our industries in New Mexico would be a good fit for China. I thought of Intel, which was in my district and eventually located a plant in China. We left China on our own and went to Hong Kong. We all were so happy to find a McDonalds after all of the Chinese food. It was delicious but we weren't accustomed to eating Chinese food for breakfast, lunch, and dinner. Mel and I stayed in Hong Kong for a few days and flew back to Hawaii for a few days before returning to New Mexico.

It was an eye-opening trip for all of us, and it helped me see the larger world and how our state functions and solves our problems. The massive scale of problems in China led me to believe that we can handle our problems in New Mexico. Our little group of five got along very well. Mel and I helped Mike Runnels when he ran successfully for district attorney in our county, and we continue to be friends. He was the coordinator of our trip, and he was always gracious, polite, and smart, and we appreciated that. Tom and Linda were nice companions, and in the Senate I later worked with Tom when he had retired from the Senate to become a lobbyist.

The China we visited no longer exists; it is now one of the world's economic leaders and holds many of the bonds that support our American debt. The Communist Party still rules in China, and there is less personal freedom than found in democratic countries. I think that the desire for more political and personal freedom will be a part of the future of China as demonstrated in Tiananmen Square.

Napoleon said, "Let China sleep, for when she wakes, she will shake the world." I think that Napoleon was right.

Trip to Japan—1989

In early November 1989 (from October 28 to November 9, 1989), with the backing and financial assistance of the United States–Japan Foundation, I joined the delegation of the National Conference of State Legislatures on a legislative exchange project to Japan. The foundation was established in 1981 for the purpose of improving the understanding between our two countries. Our delegation consisted of a single legislator each from the states of Louisiana, New Mexico, Florida, Illinois, New York, Maine, Colorado, Arizona, New Hampshire, and Nebraska. We were equally divided between Democrats and Republicans and also between state senators and state representatives. We had an equal number of men and women. Additionally we had one staff director from Idaho, two staff directors from NCSL, one interpreter, one consultant, two spouses, and two other relatives. My husband, Mel, was with us, and of course he paid for his trip. He had served in the Air Force during the Korean War and had rest and relaxation (R and R) in Japan, so he knew and loved Japan. He became the unofficial leader of the spouse group, three ladies and Mel. He made suggestions about what they should do while we were attending meetings. One day I came back to the hotel and all of the ladies were in our room having massages. I was jealous so I arranged for a massage later.

Eighteen of us traveled around Japan by bus, bullet train, and subway for two weeks. The leader of the delegation was Senator Samuel Nunez, president pro tempore of the Louisiana State Senate and also the president of the National Conference of State Legislatures. He and I were the only officials who served on the Executive Committee of the NCSL that were on the trip. This would become important for me later in the trip.

We all got to know each other quite well and shared ideas from our respective states. There was no problem with different political parties or views on

⊙ Mel and Pauline in kimonos on visit to Japan.

policy issues. The topic of our legislative exchange program was care for the elderly in the United States as compared to Japan.

We had detailed agenda packets from Kathy Brennan Wiggins, the director of international programs for NCSL. The Japan Study Tour spent three days in Tokyo, followed by visits to the prefectures (states) of Kanagawa, Kyoto, Okayama, and Hyogo. We were accompanied throughout our tour by Ms. Yukari Yamamoto.

The topic of care for the elderly was divided into a few major subcategories: alternatives to institutional care, nursing homes and services, and long-term care funding. We started in Tokyo by talking with officials from various ministries that have jurisdiction over the study tour's topic of care for the elderly. The prefecture (state) governments in Japan do not have as much authority as our state legislatures and tend to follow the direction set by the national government. From Tokyo we went by bus to Yokohama, capital of Kanagawa prefecture. We made a courtesy call on the governor and visited health institutes located in the area. In Hakone we visited the Fuji-Hakone-Iau National Park that had hot springs and unparalleled views of Mount Fuji. We had a great day with a tour guide, including a cable car ride over a volcanic gorge and a boat ride across Lake Ashinoko. It was a national holiday and quite crowded.

Kyoto was a highpoint of the trip for me, as I had studied about this city, which had been Japan's capital for more than a thousand years (794–1868) and is still the cultural capital of Japan. It was the only major Japanese city not bombed during World War II because one of General McArthur's staff had studied there and understood its value to the Japanese and to the world as a cultural heritage. We spent all day Sunday walking around the Shinto shrines and gardens and a few of the fifteen hundred Buddhist temples.

We left for Kobe as we had an appointment with the Hyogo prefectural assembly. A meeting of the entire assembly was called for our delegation visit and a luncheon was hosted in our honor. The Japanese officials were very hospitable and formal, and we exchanged gifts with a great deal of bowing and dignity.

The leader of our delegations, Senator Sammy Nunez, presented our NCSL gifts of plates and plaques. In addition, we had all brought small gifts from our states. I brought thirty-five carved Zuni bears as gifts for all the officials we met, as tokens of our state of New Mexico. My selection was also dictated by what I could pack in my suitcase that was small enough to carry. We also had been advised to bring two hundred business cards, as it is an important social custom in Japan to exchange business cards, similar to shaking hands in an introduction in the United States. I also carried little lapel pins of American flags and the state flag of New Mexico. The children enjoyed the flag pins, and I always got a big smile when I handed out pins.

Care for the elderly was our topic of discussion, and we found that the Japanese have the same major problem as the United States: the elderly population is the fastest growing segment of the population in each of our countries. In the United States the number of people over age sixty-five grew 54 percent between 1960 and 1980. Persons seventy-five and older are the fastest growing elderly population in the United States. The baby boomers in the United States had, in 2010, reached the category of elderly and the cost of health care is skyrocketing.

Japan compares quite favorably with other industrial nations with respect to health status. The Japanese people enjoy a level of general well-being that is among the highest in the world. The life expectancy for males of 74.20 and that for females of 79.78 years in 1984 were the highest in the world.

We discussed the alternatives to institutional care, nursing homes, and other services for the elderly and visited some of these in Japan. Most of the elderly are cared for by family members in the United States and Japan, but as the population grows older the costs escalate. Japan has universal health care insurance, as do other major industrial nations. This is a major issue for the United States, then and now, as we do *not* have a universal health care system, although a major health care reform bill was recently passed by the Congress and signed into law by President Barack Obama in 2010.

The cost of these plans is a large share of the gross domestic product in all of the countries that provide health care for their citizens. In the United States we presently provide care for the elderly through Medicare, Medicaid, Social Security, and other programs.

Other priority issues for the elderly include specialty care, particularly for Alzheimer's disease victims; mental health needs; and access to health care in rural areas. Also important are legal rights, notably elder abuse prevention and state ombudsman programs; indigent care; and special transportation programs. We discussed how each of our states tries to help with the care of the elderly and shared ideas for programs, but the major issue was always the cost.

We discussed and received briefing papers on a number of other issues, such as Japan-U.S. trade, Japanese local government in comparative perspective, technology policy in Japan and the United States, Japanese investment in the United States, and the meaning to the United States of Japan as a future nuclear exporter. We learned a lot from our Japanese colleagues, and we all brought home information to share about the issues we discussed and what we witnessed as we traveled through Japan.

About nine days through our tour, Senator Sammy Nunez had to return home. The staff came to me and said that since I was the only other Executive Committee member, that I would be the leader of the remainder of the tour. I was now responsible for keeping the conversations going during our meetings, presenting the gifts, and meeting with the leaders of all of the groups we interacted with during the remainder of the tour. That was twenty-one years ago, and there were not many women leaders in Japan then or now, as it was a male-dominated culture. We had a conversation with the staff and decided that this would not be upsetting to the Japanese officials as they were reaching out to the Americans and understood that the women's role was changing in our society. I assumed the leadership of the delegation and enjoyed it.

One of the most poignant events of the whole trip was an unscheduled trip to the National Atomic Museum in Hiroshima. My husband had planned to take the spouses to Hiroshima by train while we were attending meetings on health care. The ladies were enthusiastically in favor of this trip.

We had a knock on our door the night before and it was the staff indicating that we were not supposed to separate the delegation. The ladies and my husband wanted to go to the museum, and after some discussion, the schedule was rearranged and we all went to the National Atomic Museum.

When we arrived at the museum it was very quiet, even though there were large numbers of children, as it is required in Japan that every child go to the museum. We were the only Americans, and the children were staring at us as we all looked at the devastation of the atomic bomb on Hiroshima in the displays presented in the museum. The dead bodies, the sick people, the impact on the cities, and the look in the children's eyes was very emotional for me.

I was standing by myself in front of a display of "Little Boy," a replica of the A-bomb that was created in Los Alamos, New Mexico. This was the county next to mine and I had visited it numerous times. I was thinking about the creation of the nuclear weapon in New Mexico, and now I was witnessing the death and destruction that had come from the use of the bomb. President Truman made the decision to use the weapon to stop the war and save lives, and I believe it did save American lives. In front of my eyes, I saw what Dr. Robert Oppenheimer, who helped create the weapon, had predicted if the weapon was used.

At that moment, a staff person came to tell me that the director of the museum was coming to meet me, as the leader of the delegation from the United States. I was frozen in my spot in front of "Little Boy" which had been created in New Mexico, when the director appeared by my side. He was polite, formal, and we exchanged gifts and spoke of a future without such weapons and peace in the world. I expected he knew where I was from as I also gave him a little carved Zuni bear from New Mexico. He did not let on that I represented the state where the bomb was created, but of course I knew he must have made that connection.

There was a presence in that room at that moment with us, and I was focused on that moment. I have often thought of how all of that happened. I was not supposed to be the leader of the delegation, and we were not scheduled to go to the National Atomic Museum in Hiroshima to witness the results of the dropping of the atomic bomb. Yet here I was riveted to this spot. It was a moment of truth for me, when two ideas bump against each other and you can see the purpose of an act and the consequences of an action, or political decision. When decisions are made we don't always understand the outcomes, but I could not avoid knowing the results at that moment.

This encounter had a long-lasting effect on me, as I always try to think of the effect of the enactment of public policy. The act of governing is choosing and there are always consequences.

CHAPTER NINE

Capital Projects, or the Pork Bills

Tell me and I'll forget, show me and I may remember,
involve me and I'll understand.

—Chinese Proverb

Some legislators thought that their major job in Santa Fe was to bring home their share of the capital project money for their district. The capital project money comes from the severance tax bond funds and the general obligation bond funds that are submitted to the voters to approve. The latter fund, or GO bonds, generally applies to the big statewide or regional projects such as the statewide senior centers, major road repair, prison repair, hospitals, and bridges.

The amount of money varied each year based on the levels in the funds for allocation for bonds. During my time in the legislature, this money pie was split into three sections: one-third for the House, one-third for the Senate, and one-third for the governor. I believe the rule of thumb for this division was not a written rule but a custom that had been established and continued. This leads to an immediate tension between the House and the Senate based on the numbers in each house. Each senator had about two times more than each House member to put into their capital projects. I experienced quite a nice surprise in the Senate when I had $1 million for the projects in my district for one year. In the House a subcommittee of the Taxation and Revenue Committee holds the hearings and, with consultation of the sponsor, allocates the available funds, which is always voted on the last day of the session. It kept everyone's attention.

The Senate had a different procedure. All of the severance tax bills for capital projects were presented and heard in the Finance Committee. As members of that committee, we always had a little more influence, and it was also considered a choice committee because of the flow of all the bills that went through it. They were all tabled, and depending on the money available, they were prioritized by each sponsor and assembled by a staff person for the committee to vote on. It is a massive undertaking to put all of this in statutory language for one giant bill, which, as was done in the House, was voted on during the last day of the session.

The senators always took more time to debate on the floor than the House members, and one time the clock ran out. The pork bill failed before we could vote on it and that year the capital projects were not funded. As I recall that was a deliberate maneuver by Senator William Davis to prevent the vote on the capital project bill. The next time I remember this almost happening was when Senator Manny Aragon was debating, actually talking to himself and the gallery, as no senator was listening to his words. It was fifteen minutes until sine dia, or the mandated close of the session. I went over to Senator Roman Maes's seat on the floor, next to me, and said, "What is he doing and how can we stop him?" Roman said he wasn't sure, but he wanted his pork bills also, so we stood up and got about two other senators to join us and went down to the floor where Manny was standing and whispered for him to sit down. He stopped in midsentence and sat down, apparently having forgotten about the time. I have wondered if we hadn't requested him to relinquish the microphone, if we would have lost the pork for all the legislative districts again that year. There is a rule that enables a vote to stop the clock and proceed with debate. It is rarely used, because of the difficulties that could follow when debate is opened again.

Of course, all legislators consider their pork to be very important, more important than anyone else's pork, so the allocation of these bills is serious business. One of the bills that I spent a lot of time on for my district was the Sports Park Facility Bill in 1997, for $100,000. This bill was an outgrowth of a conversation I had with Frank Marquez on my patio. He said we really needed a soccer field for our kids in the county because we had about a thousand to fifteen hundred kids playing on public school fields, the former University of Albuquerque fields, and alfalfa fields in Corrales. I was aware of the need because our son, Keith, was a soccer player all through his school years. He was on the varsity team for Cibola High School. We began to plan how we could involve Rio Rancho, Bernalillo, Corrales, and Santa Ana Pueblo in the project as well as Sandoval County, which would manage any money I could bring home from the capital project funds in Santa Fe.

During my years in the legislature I began writing reports for the local newspapers called the "District 44 Report" and later, "My Corner of the Round-house," which describe what I was doing on policy and community issues. In my "District 44 Report" about the sports park, which also appeared in the *Rio Rancho Observer* in 1987, I wrote:

The Sports Park Task Force met and has made recommendations for the location of the facility which will receive $100,000 from the selling of Severance Tax Bonds by the State of New Mexico. This is the result of legislation (HB 61) which I introduced during the last session. My co-sponsors were all of the representatives in Sandoval County: Representative Roger Madalena, Representative R. W. Johnson, and Representative Delbert Sundberg; and Representative Gary Hocevar of Bernalillo county. . . .

The location is a 7.5 acre tract located just off of New Mexico 528 that is presently owned by the Rio Rancho Soccer Club. The group is willing to make the land available for public use in order to get it developed. The site recommendation, made by a task force of representatives from Corrales, Rio Rancho, and Bernalillo, has been sent to Sandoval County, which is designated as the fiscal agent for the state funds. We need to do some planning and site analysis, but I'm hoping for a minimum of three, maybe four fields. Each will have grass and a watering system.

The task force also recommended that the county monitor the project. The task force advisors include three municipalities as well as members of groups that might be using the facility. I am hoping that a good deal of the labor and landscaping for the project will be donated to stretch the state funds as far as possible. I want to thank the following members of the task force that have made the sports facility a "dream come true." The overall chairman was Frank Marquez of Corrales, who has gone on to work for Sandoval County and later Bernalillo County putting capitol projects together. He was invaluable on this project. We had three committees; the needs assessment, with John Aragon as the chairman, the site identification, selection, and cost committee, which Don Renton chaired and the organization and operation committee which was chaired by the Mayor of Corrales, Laura Warren, Rio Rancho Mayor Tom Swisstack and Mayor Ron Abousleman of Bernalillo. . . . We had about 15 people helping on this project and all of the communities took some ownership of the project. That is the best way to develop a project. When we had a ground breaking for this project the mayors were there, the political people were there and also the kids, who would actually play soccer on the fields. It was a wonderful project as everyone understood the need and helped to make the soccer fields a reality.

Another important bill that I worked on was the creation of the Petroglyph National Monument. This was a massive effort made by numerous community

❂ Pictures of petroglyphs from the proposed Petroglyph
National Monument.

groups, political entities, and the pueblos of New Mexico. My House Bill 77 was
cosponsored by many of the legislators that represented Bernalillo and Sandoval
counties, and it was referred to the Taxation and Revenue Committee and then
to Appropriations and Finance Committee. Representative Dick Minzner, one
of the cosponsors, chaired the Taxation and Revenue Committee. He had been
very helpful to me when I arrived in the House two years earlier, and I learned
to follow his lead on certain issues and bills related to finances, taxes, and legal
issues. Dick analyzed bills carefully and always understood the ramifications
for the future. He and his wife Pamela, a judge on the Supreme Court, became
friends of ours, and we still miss Pamela, who died a few years ago. Dick served
on Governor King's cabinet as the secretary of taxation and revenue, and he
continues to be involved in the politics of our state as well as practicing law.

I had a long list of people who wanted to testify on this bill in the committee, and with Dick's help the following people testified: Ike Eastvold, president, Friends of the Albuquerque Petroglyphs; Ellie Mitchell, League of Women Voters; Cliff Anderson, Open Space Advisory Board; Ken Cassutt, Sierra Club; Vince Murphy, state director for U.S. senator Jeff Bingaman; Doug Faris, U.S. National Park Service; John Gonzales, president, National Council of American Indians; Herman Agoyo, president, All Indian Pueblo Council; Albuquerque City Council president Patrick Baca; Albuquerque mayor Ken Schultz; and Mary Lou Sorenson, president, Quality of Life Coalition. It was a long morning, but they all had valuable points of view and they were well received. The committee was beginning to see the value of preserving these petroglyphs and no longer referred to them as rock graffiti; now they were discussed as an art form created on rocks.

The bill authorized the issuance of severance tax bonds for the purpose of acquiring land representing the state's commitment to the proposed petroglyph national monument; making an appropriation; declaring an emergency. The amount requested was $5.7 million, and this amount was finally shared with the Senate when it passed its version of the bill.

The U.S. Senate Bill 286 had already been introduced by Senators Jeff Bingaman and Pete Domenici with a companion bill in the House of Representatives by Congressman Steve Schiff and supported by Congressman Bill Richardson. The estimates for cost of the land were in the range of $90 million, and the distribution was for the city of Albuquerque to raise $13.8 million from a gross receipts tax, the federal government to allocate $40–50 million, and the state to contribute $6 million for land acquisition. A study in 1986 by Research Associates indicated the economic impact from the creation of the Petroglyph National Monument would be about $5 million annually from tourists coming to visit the national monument.

In January 1989, the Indian and Conservation Groups held a press conference to applaud the introduction of the bills in Congress and in Santa Fe. Herman Agoyo, chairman of the All-Indian Pueblo Council, representing New Mexico's nineteen pueblos said, "To us these petroglyphs embody our past traditions and religion, and we still use certain areas of the escarpment for sacred ceremonies that have been going on for centuries before the time of the Spanish Conquistadores and the white man." There are estimated to be fifteen thousand to seventeen thousand petroglyphs, on 6,335 acres on the escarpment and parts of the adjacent mesa and volcanoes, which is the largest concentration of rock art near a major city in the world.

In April 1989, I was invited to provide testimony before the U.S. Senate Subcommittee on Public Lands, National Parks, and Forests. Excerpts of my testimony follows:

Mr. Chairman, Senator Domenici, Senator Bingaman, and members of the committee, it is an honor to be invited to testify before you today on an issue that is of great importance to Albuquerque, the state of New Mexico, and our Nation. We have an opportunity to preserve the Petroglyphs in a National Monument that will benefit future generations of mankind indefinitely. We are very proud that Albuquerque was selected by *Newsweek* as one of America's ten "hot cities." One of the reasons given was our ambitious open space program. I quote, "Albuquerque boasts a North American rarity; a thriving present built atop a visible ancient past. Carved along the base of the volcanoes on the city's western edge are Petroglyphs dating back tens of thousands of years."

The Petroglyphs, to me, are letters that transcend time. They are messages of life, hunger, war, birth, sickness, and joy. They are rock secrets that we can share with the past and the future. Thank you for this opportunity to testify before your committee today.

Many others were also invited to testify, and we finally passed the legislation in Congress, Santa Fe, and Albuquerque, that created the Petroglyph National Monument. It was an effort that bubbled up from the community to capture so many of us to help achieve this goal. I feel happy when I pass the Petroglyph sign or visit the monument with tourist friends or family, as I remember the monumental effort so many people made to accomplish the preservation of these letters from the past.

A lot of time is spent on presenting capital project bills bringing up community members to testify and working with the committee to get your share of the available funds for your district. During my years in the House and the Senate I've brought home for my district more than $3 million for senior centers, the Rio Rancho library, the Corrales library, Bernalillo water and sewer projects, road blacktopping for Corrales and Bernalillo, improvements to Northern Boulevard in Rio Rancho, an East Mountain community center sound system, a bicycle trail for the East Mountains, Loma Larga Road for Corrales (year after year to get enough money for the project), Bernalillo youth center, Rio Rancho park rehabilitation, Rio Rancho Sabana Grande pool, Rio Rancho Fire Department ambulances, Bernalillo remodeling for Roosevelt School, playground flood control for Carroll Elementary School, open space for Placitas, and a water tank for the Placitas village water system. Later the Albuquerque Public Schools developed the cluster system and requested funds for the schools in our clusters. I helped with the irrigation ponds for the wastewater system for Corrales Elementary School and the

✪ Ground breaking for a new water project for the town
of Bernalillo with Senator Steve Stoddard and Damian
Rinaldi, son of Maria Rinaldi.

computers for Cibola High School. The Rio Rancho school system, which I helped to develop as a separate school district, was always in need of help with their infrastructure.

My system for developing the list for capital projects was to visit with all of the municipalities, counties, and schools that were in my district and request their priorities for the next legislative session. I also worked on the larger projects such as the Paseo del Norte Bridge, Northern Boulevard in Rio Rancho, Coronado Monument, Unser Boulevard, fencing for the open space in Placitas, and the intergenerational center for Santa Ana Pueblo in 1990. It was more difficult to determine the needs of the unincorporated areas and try to help. Sandoval County was helpful, and as the growth of Rio Rancho brought in more tax dollars, the county developed projects that I was able to help them with in the legislature. These were multiple-year projects and requests for money such as the new Sandoval County courthouse, which was completed in 2010. Debbie Hays, the county manager for a lot of the time I was in the legislature, was very helpful and knowledgeable about the needs of Sandoval County. Debbie also got along well with all of the officials in the municipalities in my district, so it was helpful to coordinate with her. She and her husband, Brad, live in Corrales, and we have worked together on a lot of political issues over the years. Brad was a former State Democratic Party chairman and also chairman of the Sandoval County Democratic Party.

A few of the projects are still clear in my memory because of the people involved and how important it was for them to come to the state legislature and get some help in their community. One of these was the intergenerational project for the Santa Ana Pueblo. The idea was to construct a building that would house a preschool and a senior center so that there could be interaction between the two. The storyteller dolls that are created by the Pueblo of Cochiti represented in clay the kind of interaction that I had envisioned. This was in the late 1980s, before we voted on the Indian Gaming Compact in 1997, and the pueblo administrators told me they had never received any help from the state before this time. I had visited the pueblo and appreciated the need for this new building and told them I would try to help them.

On the day the bill was heard in committee, about twenty-five members from the pueblo came to testify. I loved it, as there were little children who spoke about a new preschool and seniors who talked about a place to visit with each other and tell the children stories. They gave me a list of the officials of the village and I introduced the governor, Eligio Montoya; the administrator, Roy Montoya; and the other officials. When I got to the war chief, everyone in the room applauded. The presentation ended with a song from the children. I had some legislators tell me later that they had never seen a pueblo group come to testify before. I asked Senator Steve Stoddard of Los Alamos, who represented the pueblo in the Senate, to help with this bill, and we were able to allocate about $100,000 to help get this building project started. Santa Ana was always a pleasure to work with, and we still have friends there that we continue to visit during special occasions.

Another bill that was fun for me was the Sandoval County Flood Control Authority legislation, creating this new governmental entity as the population growth in Rio Rancho required a lot of attention to flood control. We had companion bills to create the Sandoval County Flood Control Authority and I was carrying the initial funding bill in the House. The state engineer, Steve Reynolds, was my expert witness for this legislation. Reynolds had been the state engineer for more than twenty-five years and was recognized as the water expert for New Mexico and the southwest region of the country. We testified in two committees, and he was treated as if he were royalty by the committee members. At the end of the second committee meeting, after they had voted a do pass motion, the committee chairman said, "Mr. Reynolds, is there anything else we can help you with?" I wished I could clone Steve Reynolds and take him with me for some of my other bills. He was an icon in our state, and his word was trusted by the legislators. When he died, Governor King knew it would be difficult to fill his shoes.

The Rio Rancho Senior Center grew so fast that eventually there was no more land to expand the center on Meadowlark Road. I recall that Amrep Southwest, the major development company of Rio Rancho, donated the land and the city built the center. I visited often as it was a great place to have lunch with the seniors and talk with them about their concerns; also my fishing club buddies met there on Mondays. I helped with a couple of

✪ My fishing buddies from the Rio Rancho Senior Center Fishing Club at Fenton Lake.

✪ Pauline and members of the Fishing Club meet with Governor Garrey Curruthers to get help with Fenton Lake.

additions, kitchen equipment, and the last thing was more land donated by Amrep Southwest for a large parking lot. I found a picture of the ground-breaking for the parking lot, and as I looked at the picture, I realized that a lot of the people in the picture, who were my friends, have died. The senior center continues to flourish with lots of programs. I remember Henry Engle, who helped start the first senior center at Sabana Grande, and all the other seniors that set the stage for the community that Rio Rancho has become. It has been twenty-five years since I began representing Rio Rancho in Santa Fe and now it is the third largest city in New Mexico. I think the early residents who came from all over the United States to make a better life for themselves and their children would be proud to see what a thriving city it is today. A new school district, a new city hall, a new library, Intel, Hewlett Packard, a University of New Mexico campus, and about eighty thousand people have all appeared in the last twenty years in Rio Rancho.

Susan Rinaldi was a teacher at Carroll Elementary School in the town of Bernalillo. She would bring her class and other children up to visit the legislature frequently, as I had always invited her and any other classes to visit as a part of their education. Susan invited me to speak to her class one day, and I came before lunch and they were fidgety. I said that it would be great when they could get out on the playground. But I quickly learned that they couldn't use their playground in the winter because the ground was not level, and snow, water, and mud collected everywhere. During the next legislative session the children came to Santa Fe with a power point presentation to request help for the playground rehabilitation. Susan Rinaldi and Ray Romero helped those students understand how to improve things in their own environment. Perhaps one of those children will one day serve in the legislature. The Rinaldi family continue to be friends, and recently I went with Justin Rinaldi, his sister Margaret, his daughter Michelle, and his niece Maria on a train trip to Santa Fe to visit the new History of New Mexico Museum.

John Rinaldi, Susan's husband, is a former Sandoval county commissioner and a former professor of the College of Education at the University of New Mexico. The family has always worked to help make things better in the town of Bernalillo.

The last capital project I want to highlight are the road memorials, which I used for two years, 1990 and 1991. These were memorials requesting money for roads from the state transportation department. They were used in Bernalillo and Corrales to blacktop dirt roads in the rural areas. In Corrales a number of the residents did not want their roads blacktopped because they didn't want the traffic to increase. I asked the village to do a survey of the residents on the roads they selected to blacktop prior to agreeing to do the job. Mayor Laura Warren sent out the following letter to the residents of the selected roads.

Representative Pauline Eisenstadt has secured money for the black-topping of some roads in Corrales. Your road has been selected as a possibility for this project. Representative Eisenstadt has requested a consensus of a majority of the residents on each road as to whether or not they would like to have their road blacktopped. If a majority of the residents on each road do not want blacktopping, other roads will be chosen. Please return this letter with your preference for surface material for your road to the Village offices by March 7, 1990.

I had secured money for three to four roads in each of these communities at about fifty thousand dollars a mile, they told me, depending on the length of the road. They all agreed except Dixon Road in Corrales, which was split. The western half wanted the road blacktopped and the eastern half did not. So now you know why Dixon road is only half paved. Later, a resident told me that it was not fair, because the renters not the owners voted not to pave. I thought that the consensus was a great idea to satisfy everyone, but that is never possible.

Capital projects are important to the communities I represented, and I worked hard to help all of them, but they are not the reason I ran for office. I've always been concerned about public policy, and issues such as education, children's welfare, economic development, information technology, and the allocation of the resources of the state that affect the daily lives of the people. My passion was always for the policy development and planning for the future, while navigating through the political arena.

CHAPTER TEN

My Time in the
House of Representatives
1985–1993

For those to whom much is given, much is required.
And when at some future date the high court of history
sits in judgment on each of us, recording whether in our
brief span of service we fulfilled our responsibilities to
the state, our success or failure, in whatever office we
hold, will be measured by the answers to four questions:

First, were we truly people of courage?
Second, were we truly people of judgment?
Third, were we truly people of integrity?
Finally, were we truly people of dedication?

—John F. Kennedy

The state budget is the major issue the legislature needs to decide each year. The budget is where the decisions are made about how the state's treasure will be spent and the amounts are determined by the governor and the legislature. Through use of the veto pen to cut out a funding category entirely, the governor has the last say; however a governor can't cut what is not included in the budget. The dance between the governor and the legislature continues in every session and with every governor.

As I write this chapter, it is three days before the opening day of the 2010 legislative session. KNME, our local public television company, has invited me and three other former legislators to provide comments for Governor Richardson's State of the State address as we sit in the Albuquerque studio. I believe this will be in real time and the audience can sit in their homes or offices and see and hear the speech on their computers. What a technological miracle this is. The excitement of the first day is palatable in the chamber of the House of Representatives. I always enjoyed opening day, but this time I'm glad that I don't have to face a $500 million deficit in the revenues for the state budget as a member of the House or Senate. The choices are very difficult; either raise taxes or cut programs dramatically, and I expect the governor will choose to do a little of each of these options. All around the country, the same problem is happening because of the near collapse of the economy. The economy appears to be coming back, although unemployment is still high, and therefore individual spending is still too low for our gross receipts taxes to provide their large portion of the state's revenue.

During all of my terms in the House and the Senate, I served with four governors: Toney Anaya, Democrat; Garrey Carruthers, Republican; Bruce King, Democrat; and Gary Johnson, Republican. I always listened carefully to their opening day speeches as they stated what they wanted to focus on during their terms in office. The first speech after their election was the one that pointed in the direction of their major areas of concern and what they hoped to achieve during their term as governor of New Mexico. The political party affiliation would often tell you which direction the governors would take during a crisis like this one, with the $500 million deficit.

This particular financial crisis is the biggest one since the Great Depression of the 1930s, and it will take every innovation and every idea to come up with the money to maintain the state's programs for education, social services, police protection, and all the other areas of state provided services. On the other side of the issue is the way to raise revenue through increased taxes. One suggestion is to rescind the law that removed taxes from food and drugs. It is difficult to raise taxes during a recession because the business community is having a hard time, and we are dependent on them to create more jobs. In the past, there were corners in state government that had retained unspent revenues, or capital project money that had not been spent, or money for new positions that not been filled yet, but all of these corners have already been swept clean.

On opening day of the legislature, the leaders of the House and the Senate appoint about four members from each chamber to go up to the governor's office to escort him and his wife to the House of Representatives for his speech. It is a little bit of ceremony that I participated in for all the governors that I served with during my terms of office. This procedure was usually a formality, a happy time, and we would joke with the governors on the way down in the elevator to the floor of the House. When I was appointed to escort Governor Gary Johnson to the chamber I found that he had an interesting little cheering squad for him as he emerged from the governor's office into the hall where his elevator was located. The hallway was lined with all of his staffers, and they were shouting "Gary, Gary, Gary" in cadence to a football cheer. I thought at the time, this legislative session has more consequences than a game. Our policies affect lives dramatically, but that was his staff's choice to cheer him on like that, and he was our mountain-climbing governor.

When we arrived in the chamber the sergeant of arms of the House, Gilbert Baca, would shout, "Mr. Speaker, the governor has arrived to address the members of the House and the Senate." He had a booming voice and everyone liked him, as he was always available to help with our needs on the floor during the session. The sergeant of arms got everyone's attention and the noise quieted down. Then the introductions began, and this would include former and present officials, and particularly the members of the Supreme Court, the third branch of government, who would be sitting on a podium above the governor. I thought that was symbolic as their words were law in any dispute between any of parties or laws that that were judged to be unconstitutional. Our system of government works because we trust the checks and balances provided by the courts.

The media was always there, and they were intent on getting the governor's speech and his major focus correctly. They also wanted reaction from some of the rest of us on the floor. I have sat on the floor and sat in the television booth in Santa Fe and also in Albuquerque. The analysis is quite different. As I provide analysis for Governor Richardson's speech in 2010, I have a more relaxed view of the ideas and issues. I know the bills will be amended and changed before we see them again in law, if they pass. Primarily, I'm removed from the fury of the discussion, and I don't have to vote every step of the way that a bill takes to become a law.

The governors have different relationships with the legislature depending on their past experience and whether they have served in the legislature themselves, or held other political office. The governor that I worked with who had the best understanding of the legislature was Governor Bruce King, who was a former Speaker of the House. Governor King would come down to the House of Representatives floor during the session to visit with us, and of course, to round up votes for his ideas. I worked with him on a lot of the children's issues and business issues, such as prenatal care, child abuse, education, and tax credits for Intel's expansion. In his autobiography, Governor King described himself as a moderate who cared about the people in the state and believed that government should provide some of the services to help them live better lives. I found a lot to like about his policies the longer I stayed in elected office and the more pragmatic I became. I'm a reformer at heart, and I've always wanted to make things work properly, which prompted my introduction of ethics legislation in the House for three sessions in a row. I did not succeed in passing the legislation that I had proposed, but the legislature did begin to understand the need for the ethics legislation and small steps were taken in my last year in the House. Ethics legislation is an ongoing process.

It appears one infraction can be altered and another need is then apparent. These issues are found in every state in our union and require constant vigilance. Often it is necessary to start with a small part of the solution and keep on adding to the solution as a complete fix for a problem is very difficult. The process of making laws is a very difficult one and almost all the issues I tackled had opposition from lots of lobbyists. They frequently had good points that needed to be considered.

An example of a bill that had immediate support from most everyone was the Grandparent's Visitation Bill that I passed in 1987. A woman in Albuquerque named Marilyn Shearer was a fifty-five-year-old grandmother who had waged a long-term court battle for the right to visit her eight-year-old grandson after her son had passed away. She had been shut out of her grandson's life by the new husband and her former daughter-in-law. Marilyn said they told her, "We have our own family now and don't want to have anything to do with you any more." Marilyn Shearer formed a support group called Grandparents Are Indeed Necessary, or GAIN. This group called me and invited me to come to one of their meetings, and although we had no grandchildren at the time, I clearly understood the problem. If there has been a major disruption in the family, it is very important for the child to continue the bond with the grandparents. I agreed to sponsor the legislation. Judge Susan Conway, who presided over the Second Judicial District in Albuquerque, helped draft the new law.

The new law allows grandparents to petition for visitation rights if a child is adopted, or if a child has lived with a grandparent for at least six months and is taken away by a parent, the grandparents may seek visitation rights. The new law is an important one for New Mexico, because extended families are more prevalent here than other areas of the country, and children of parents in their teens or early twenties are often raised by their grandparents. The grandparents see the new law as a big victory for their rights. Judge Conway thought it was also a big victory for the grandchildren. Marilyn Shearer was very appreciative of my efforts on behalf of this legislation, and every now and then someone I don't recognize will come over to me at a meeting or a social event and thank me for helping them keep their grandchildren in their lives.

This bill passed without much controversy but it still required going through committees in the House and the Senate and having votes on the floors of both houses. That is why only 350–400 bills out of the 3,000 introduced into the typical sixty-day session pass into law. The committee system is very important in vetting the bills and making sure they amend out the problems or put in something that will help the bill. But, as becomes obvious, it is a lot easier to kill a bill than to pass one. The role of the lobbyist becomes very important, as they can help or hurt your bill at every juncture. The makeup of the committee is also important, and a legislator always has to do their "laundry list," that is, vote counting, before their bill comes to the committee for a vote. An effort is made to talk to members of the committee and explain the bill, count your votes, and then your votes need to be in the room for the vote. Most bills are pretty routine, changing or adding something in a governmental department, changing penalties for minor offenses, creating study committees, or capital projects bills. About 85 percent of the bills that eventually pass receive a majority of the votes if they reach the floor, but the other 15 percent are hard fought battles. I would usually cosponsor about thirty bills, particularly the interim committee bills and bills of friends with whom I often agreed. I would try to limit myself to about fifteen to eighteen significant bills that I would have to fight for. These took a lot of planning and effort to succeed.

The legislative sessions are whirlwinds of activity after the first week of organizing. It takes a new member a while to figure out how the process works. The bills have to be prepared by the Legislative Council Service in the proper form and printed, duplicated, and distributed on the floor of each chamber by the sergeant of arms and his staff. The interim committee bills have been prepared by the staff before the session, and the sponsors can begin getting signatures of cosponsors. The first few days require the organizing for the direction that the rest of the session will take. The bills are referred to committees to be heard, debated, tabled, or sent to the next committee, depending on the votes of the first committee.

The Legislative Council Service is key to the functioning of the legislative activities, and Paula Tackett has been the director since the death of Clay Buchanan in 1988. Paula was very professional and was respected by the legislators of the House and the Senate; I always enjoyed visiting with her about the issues I was concerned about. Her staffs were the people that we all depended on to prepare our legislation and have it ready for introduction on the floor of each chamber. I recall receiving help from Sharlene Shoemaker on a lot of my children and family issues. She was smart, efficient, and could draft a bill to achieve the desired goal. Most legislation is a magnet for amendments. The committee system is focused on elimination of problems from bills or removing unintended consequences through amendments. The lobbyists can be of great help, but they are also very skillful at hijacking and killing bills.

For controversial legislation that required simple and concise language, I requested the help of Stuart Bluestone. He was able to help me put difficult concepts into appropriate language for the ethics bills and later in the Senate with the evolution bill. Stuart went on to work as deputy director for two attorney generals, Patricia Madrid and Gary King, and he continues to be a man that I admire and count as a friend.

I had the help of many other competent people on the staff of the Legislative Council Service over the years. As an advisory member of the Legislative

Council Service, I appreciated their assistance in making the process of drafting bills work so well, so that the elected officials could perform their duties for the citizens of the state. The Legislative Council Library is a wonderful resource for the history of legislation, elected members, leaders, dates of governor's terms, remodeling of the state capitol, and a variety of other legislative activities. Tracey Kimball is the director, as I write this memoir, and she has been very helpful with information I requested and also enthusiastic about a woman's view of the Roundhouse.

After the bills have been drafted, introduced on the floor, and assigned to committees, the work begins. In the House, I served on a number of committees including Appropriations and Finance, Judiciary, Consumer and Public Affairs, and Education. I chaired the Rules Committee and also served as the elected Majority Caucus chairman. The meetings are scheduled so that the major committees that have most of the bills to review don't conflict with each other, and members can attend to their responsibilities on a number of committees.

The pace of the session picks up very quickly. I would get to the capitol at 8:00 a.m., go to my office, drop my coat and brief case, and leave for a meeting. In the Senate, my major committee was the Senate Finance Committee and that met in the afternoon, but as the bills piled up, it began to meet all day. Toward the end of the session, the Senate would meet all day on the floor to hear the bills and the House would do the same. The House was more orderly. They kept to a schedule and there was not a lot of debate on the floor. The votes are electronic, and the outcome is clear immediately. The House members frequently referred to the senators as prima donnas, because they talked so much on the floor of the Senate and didn't leave time for the House bills to get a hearing on the floor at the end of the session. The senators thought the House members introduced too many bills that were not necessary, and they felt no obligation to hear them all. I was one of very few who had served in the House and the Senate, so I fully understood the point of view from each chamber. At the end of the session, it helped if you had a colleague in each house who could get your bills on the floor for a vote.

It became difficult to attend the committee meetings, present bills in the Senate, and pay attention to floor votes, all at the same time. The last ten days are a marathon race to get it all done before the conclusion of the session. I always rented a condo for the session and went home on Friday night, returning on Sunday afternoon, except for the last ten days when I had to stay full time in Santa Fe. By the time the end was in sight, we were working around the clock. During the sixty-day sessions, many of us had colds halfway through. I really enjoyed having the school children come up in buses to visit the legislature, and they frequently had the ubiquitous runny nose. They shared their runny noses and their hugs and I started to sneeze and cough, and I'm sure I shared that with those around me. The building had a lot of us together for long periods of time, and I calculate about one-third were sick at the end of the session. One time, I had to go home because it was really bad, but usually I started to take some cold remedy and tried to get more sleep. It was exciting, and we all got caught up in trying to pass our legislation and worked very hard to achieve the best outcome for our constituents as well as the welfare of the state.

There have been efforts to reform the legislature and tinker with the number of days for the sessions, when the sessions are held, prefiling of legislation (which we did accomplish), and paying legislators. Some we could accomplish while some would require a constitutional change. The interim committee I served on to reform the legislature could not agree on much. We got help from the National Conference of State Legislatures. They sent us a comparison of how other states tried to solve the problems of the last few days, and they were all different. Some were full-time legislatures, some met every other year, and all of them had trouble reforming or changing. Santa Fe in winter is not the best time for all of us to be there because of the driving, the weather, and the constant illness. But the old-timers are used to it, and they said, "It is too expensive in Santa Fe in the summer and the tourists have all the hotel rooms." Originally we met in the winter because we were a farming and ranching state, and the work slows in the winter. That is no longer the case, but custom prevails.

The job of Majority Caucus chairman is to organize the meetings of the Democratic members of the legislature as requested by the leaders and to set the agenda for the meetings. The leaders were elected for two years, and there were always battles for at least some of the positions. During my years in the Roundhouse the top leadership positions were held primarily by Speaker Raymond Sanchez in the House and Senator Manny Aragon as president pro tem of the Senate. The first Speaker I served with was Gene Samberson, and Dick Minzner was majority leader. The majority whip was Representative Ben Luján. During my terms as Majority Caucus chairwoman I served with Speaker Sanchez, Majority Leader Toby Michael, and Majority Whip Ben Luján. The seniority system was a factor in leadership and committee chairs but not always. In the House the Democrats always held a significant majority, with the Republicans usually lagging far behind, something like forty-five to twenty-seven. But, there were always a number of conservative Democrats that would vote with the Republicans on some issues that they felt reflected their districts.

As the Majority Caucus chairwoman, my job was to organize meetings that the leadership felt were necessary, set the agenda, and notify all the members to attend. We would have a meeting before the session, particularly when we were voting for the leadership positions. During the legislative sessions we would have them weekly, or more often if something was critical.

I would always bring the most knowledgeable person in state government to help inform the members about the issues we were discussing. For example, if it was the state budget, I would bring the state budget director to the caucus; for taxes, I would request the secretary of taxation and revenue; for health care issues, the secretary of health and human services. As a former school teacher, it seemed obvious to me that we needed the best information in order to make good decisions about the issues of importance to the state. One of the House leaders came to me one day and he said, "Pauline, why are you bringing in all of these people to the caucus?" I responded that I thought the members needed to have the information so they could decide how to vote. The leader said, "No they don't, we'll tell them how to vote." This was a holdover from the past when the patron system was functioning in New Mexico. For some of us in the caucus, that was no longer a satisfactory way to function in an elected position. I continued to bring experts into the caucus to explain the issues, and I hoped it informed the members before the votes were taken.

As caucus chairwoman, I was one of the elected leaders, and I felt it was part of my responsibility to help our members function well. I recommended that we try the buddy system with office assignments, with older more experienced members helping the new members. That didn't receive a positive response. They said that they had to learn their way around, and the new legislators needed to do the same thing. Some of the new legislators were staying late at night trying to answer their mail, and I helped draft some letters that could be adapted to a large number of issues. I had requests for those sample letters for many years.

When I disagreed with something in the caucus I would voice my opinion and try to convince others, but if I was outvoted I would usually try to support the majority. Sometimes, I would disagree and let them know that they could not count on my vote because it would not represent the will of my district. Trying to pass legislation requires a lot of votes, and it becomes important to get help from your colleagues.

As a result there is a lot of compromise on the difficult issues. I remember telling a colleague that I would give him my vote in the committee, even if I did not support the bill, so they could give it a larger hearing, but not to count on my vote on the floor vote. There were a few times when a senator told me that he could not vote for my bill, but he would take a walk on the floor vote, so it would not count as a no vote. These were some of the ways that we tried to help our colleagues move legislation forward that was important to them for their districts. These were some of the compromises that were made to help one another manage to get along in a group.

Some people think there is never room for compromise, and those people will not be able to function as productive lawmakers, because there is not one way to solve a problem but many. My preference was to solve problems

✪ Pauline chairing a committee hearing in the House of Representatives.

by reforming and changing the whole system, but that becomes very difficult as I found out with the ethics legislation I introduced a number of times.
The incremental changes takes more time, but gives comfort to people as they
can adjust to small changes rather than adapt to the larger ones. I believe the
health care reform put forward by President Obama and the Congress in 2010,
which I support, may have to adapt to some incremental changes instead of
the whole system at one time.

I enjoyed the role of caucus chairwoman during the four years that I held
that position. I learned a lot from the leadership and was included in meetings with the governors and the strategy meetings regarding the Senate as the

sessions came to the end and bargaining between the House and the Senate began, before the endgame with the governors and their veto pens.

Governor Carruthers, whom I respected for trying to keep the welfare of the state in the forefront of his administration, started to have Friday afternoon parties for the leadership of both the House and the Senate. These were bipartisan get-togethers, but this didn't last too long, because at the end of the week we wanted to talk to each other or go home and get a break from the Roundhouse gossip mill. It was a good idea but perhaps since it was on the governor's turf, in his office, not a neutral setting, the Democrats felt he was in charge and weren't comfortable. Governor Carruthers's tenure in office was pretty smooth. Of course, we did not always agree on the budget and the directions he was taking on some issues; however, he did listen to the legislature about our concerns. He hired Maralyn Budke as his chief of staff, and I think that made a big difference in his ability to function with the legislative body, as she was the previous staff director of the Legislative Finance Committee. She recently passed away and will be missed by the many people she worked with during her career in public service, myself included.

I want to include some excerpts from my "District 44 Report" that was published in the *Rio Rancho Observer* and the *Corrales Comment* in April 1987 because it relates the flavor of what was happening in Santa Fe. I wrote these after each session so the people in my district would have a better idea of my activities and what was happening in Santa Fe. When I was in the Senate, I would try to send a letter updating my constituents about my legislative initiatives and they were very appreciative. But I found that the pace of work during the sessions was so much that usually I would need to have some time at home to wind down from the frenzy to compose my thoughts and report about the activity later.

> The 1987 Legislative session is over and we are all happy to be home again with our families and friends. The last week is always the most hectic and uncertain. Legislation passes or fails sometimes with minutes to spare before the session adjourns at noon on Saturday. There were a number of areas in which compromise was the necessary ingredient for success during the last week. These areas are always the appropriation levels, revenue amounts, capital outlay, and road projects.
>
> House Bill 2, which is the State appropriation bill, was in a conference committee up until Friday night, the spending level is dependent on the revenues available. Governor Garrey Carruthers requested fee increases on motor vehicles, a gas tax, eliminating rebates on food and medicine for another year, keeping the Federal windfall to $59 million for a total of about $160 million in overall tax increases. These

measures (except the windfall) were included in Senate Bills 652 and 653 which were finally approved in each house with bipartisan support. House Bill 2, the Capital outlay projects, and House Bill 762 (the road projects) were all finally agreed on and passed Saturday morning, with bi-partisan support.

The major issue facing the state continues to be the falling revenue from the oil and gas industry and the mining industry. We must wean ourselves away from our dependence on the severance tax dollars and develop our economy through new avenues such as tourism and jobs from the high tech industries. We are all hoping that the five centers of technical excellence will prove to be successful and provide some leadership in these areas.

The Grandparent Visitation Bill passed and the governor has already signed this legislation. The Door to Door Sales bill has passed, which will allow a three day "cooling off" period for any purchase over $25. The cooling off period will allow you to think about your purchase and change your mind if you didn't understand the contract. Campaign Reform and the Bottle bill were two issues that did not pass and I believe we need them both. Tomorrow is another day and after some rest with my family, I will look forward to visiting with you and hearing your opinions about the Legislative session.

It is interesting to compare the results of the 1987 session with 2010. The problems of the budget now are a lot harder to solve as the amount of the revenue shortfall is between $350–400 million. Our Republican governor Garrey Carruthers was raising taxes and cutting spending, which is the only way to resolve these problems, by using all the available methods to reach a balanced budget. This was written twenty-three years ago and the problems are similar, but the growth of the state's population and the economy has increased the scale of the problems.

An article in the *Albuquerque Journal* in February 20, 1989, caught my eye and motivated me to try to push for passage of the New Mexico Unfair Practices Act. The headline said, "Telephone Scams Called $1 Billion-a-Year Rip-Off." The *Journal* noted that a coalition of business, consumer, and government groups had exposed the problem of con artists promising prizes, penny stocks, and gold to bilk consumers out of more than $1 billion a year through deceptive telephone sales practices.

The coalition had launched a campaign to increase public awareness of the fraud, urging consumers to exercise more caution and skepticism when dealing with telephone solicitations. "If it's too good to be true, if it sounds like a quick and easy deal, it's probably a fraud," said Ron Weber, president of the American Telemarketing Association, an industry group. The coalitions said the most frequent scams are prize offers, penny stocks, credit repair, and business-to-business fraud. Our older son Todd was working for the *Nashville Independent* newspaper when he did an in-depth story on a travel scam that sold trips to the Bahamas. He was nominated for a Pulitzer Prize for that story, and I figured that if I could do something to help New Mexico citizens, maybe he would share his nomination with me.

House Bill 177, Relating to Telephone Solicitation Sales, was introduced in 1989, and eventually after careful scrutiny and a few amendments, it passed. This bill attracted lobbyists from the telephone industry and the National Direct Sellers Association from Washington. They were interested in passing something to eliminate the scam artists and not create unintended consequences for their industries. Bill Garcia with U.S. West Communications, John Badal with AT&T from Phoenix, and the government affairs director from the National Direct Sellers Association became valued assistants and helped me amend this bill to satisfy all of the objections. Bill Garcia became cabinet secretary for economic development under Governor Bruce King, while John Badal later became the president of Comcast. I enjoyed working with all of them and understood the value of the extra help in passing good legislation.

The law says it shall be unlawful to use a prerecorded message to attempt to sell goods or services unless there is an existing business relationship between the individuals and the person being called consents to hear the prerecorded message. Telephone solicitors, to be legal, also

1. must promptly disclose the name of the sponsor and the primary purpose of the call;
2. must not use the guise of research or a survey when the real intent of the call is to sell goods or services;
3. must disclose, before commitment by the customer, all costs, terms, conditions, payment plans, and any extra charges;
4. must call between 9 a.m. and 9 p.m.;
5. must use only automatic dialing equipment that immediately releases the line when the party receiving the call disconnects;
6. must not ask for credit card numbers until and unless the customer has committed to buy something and expresses a desire to use a credit card.

Violators of these rules should be reported to the Consumer Protection Division of the attorney general's office. There were a few newspaper articles describing this legislation, and I heard from the attorney general's office when they received complaints, but I'm not sure that the public really has a good understanding of these issues. It works because the New Mexico Unfair Practices Act, NMSA 1978, was amended by this law, and the violation may result in the issuance of orders for injunctive relief and restitution to consumers as well as the imposition of civil penalties of up to five thousand dollars per willful violation. When complaints are filed with the attorney general, the people running these shady businesses receive a letter about the fines and the civil penalties and that gets the attention of the scam artists. We were in the forefront of the states in protecting our citizens from these consumer frauds. This bill passed unanimously in the House, and I believe it did quite well in the Senate also; the governor signed it into law. With a lot of help, I think this legislation has greatly reduced the number of phone scams in New Mexico.

Since telecommunications has changed so much and lots of people don't have land lines anymore and use cell phones and computers to communicate, I expect the scam artists will figure out a way to develop scams through the Internet. This will be a problem for this generation of legislators to solve.

I was very active and productive in 1989. I was able to put money in the budget for the Prevention of Teenage Pregnancy; introduce the Antiterrorism Act, which passed in 1990; and cosponsor the Drug Precursor Act with Gary King. That bill puts precursor drugs that are used to make methamphetamines on the controlled substance list. This was an attempt to restrict the meth labs that were springing up all over the state. It was a step in the right direction, but as the problem is still with us today, I hope more will be done to prevent these drug labs. The people who take meth drugs have major health problems that the state will have to take care of in the future. I always try to find ways to prevent these kinds of problems, since I discovered that 70 percent of the inmates in the jails had drug problems and a similar number had been abused as children.

Representative Gary King and I became friends when we sat beside each other on the Judiciary Committee and worked together on a number of issues. Gary King was a smart, likeable, and compassionate young man that we continued to help in his career for higher office. We cohosted parties for him in Corrales when he ran for Congress in the southern district and when he ran for attorney general in 2008. He is a man of integrity. New Mexico has benefited from his talent and also that of his wife Yolanda King.

The following was a news release from October 10, 1989:

> Representative Pauline Eisenstadt, selected as one of 50 top women elected officials in the nation to participate in Strategic Leadership '90, a landmark leadership conference on October 12–15 at Harvard University's John F. Kennedy School of Government, sponsored by the Women's Campaign Research Fund and Harvard's Institute of Politics.
>
> "We're proud that Pauline Eisenstadt, as one of the nation's best and brightest women leaders today, will be joining us for Strategic

⚙ Pauline with colleague and friend, Representative Gary King, presently the New Mexico attorney general.

Leadership '90," said WCRF Executive Director Jane Danowitz. The top women candidates of the 1990s know the modern route to success is twofold: understanding the ins-and-outs of the high-tech campaign process, and knowing how to use their public office and political experience to be a leader on the critical policy issues facing their state and nation.

"I'm honored to be part of Strategic Leadership '90," said Pauline Eisenstadt, "and look forward to taking advantage of this unique opportunity to join with other key women leaders across the country to improve the quality of leadership and government in our state and nationwide."

This meeting at Harvard was the first one that I attended with so many other women that held elective office all over the country. We shared our issues in our respective states and talked about fundraising, polling, media relations, and policy development strategies. We had experts from both the Republican and Democratic perspective and discussed issues such as taxes, foreign trade, and health care. It was a big eye-opener for those of us from the smaller states like New Mexico, Idaho, and New Hampshire. A number of the women that I met at this meeting are now in congress and became governors of their states. We kept a loose network and sent campaign contributions to each other along

○ The John F. Kennedy School of Government at Harvard University with
my classmate Lawrence Rael, summer of 1991.

with wishes for further political success. This conference and others like it were
efforts to encourage women to compete and participate in the political arena
and provide some of the necessary tools to do a job. After attending a few of
these meetings, I began to think about establishing something like this in New
Mexico and made a couple of efforts at creating an Institute for Public Service
at the University of New Mexico. The first effort was with Professor Lee Brown,
chairman of the Department of Public Administration. We met with the provost
and he was interested, but then he left the university and our efforts were not
successful. Professor Brown was a big supporter of the effort but the bureau-
cracy and the need for funding proved difficult challenges to surmount.

I continued with the idea when I was in the Senate and proposed that the
Institute of Public Service become a part of the Institute of Public Law, which
was directed by Paul Nathanson. Before the session in 1999, Paul and I visited
with the leadership of Intel and Sandia Labs to explain the need to provide
training for elected officials in our state in areas of the environment, technology, and budgeting and revenues. They were supportive and each provided
checks of one thousand dollars, to indicate their support for the creation of an
Institute of Public Service. I was hoping to get an amount of money to get it
started from the legislative session and then assist with the fundraising in the
community to develop the mission.

My second effort was successful in the legislature, and we were able to
include a small amount of money for the University of New Mexico to get this

effort off the ground. Paul Nathanson had prepared a budget. I presented the bill before the Senate Finance Committee and showed the checks from Intel and Sandia Labs as evidence of the private sector support. Senate Bill 67 was an act making an appropriation to establish the Institute of Public Service at the University of New Mexico. The bill said that the expenditure of the money was for the purpose of establishing the Institute of Public Service to improve the understanding, policymaking, and administration of government by providing nonpartisan training, research, and technical assistance to public officials and community leaders, and promoting civics education and citizen involvement in the political process. In the final Senate Appropriations bill we received $300,000 from the legislature.

We thought that we had jumped the hurdles and would be in a position to provide training similar to that I had received at Harvard, but we were wrong. Governor Gary Johnson vetoed our legislation because he was opposed to any new programs that cost money. I refunded the checks to Intel and Sandia Labs with great disappointment, and I put this idea aside for the future. New Mexico needs to have some training for our elected officials to perform their duties to benefit our state, and I sincerely hope that an Institute of Public Service will be created one day.

Three years later, in 1991, I received a fellowship to attend the Program for Senior Executives in State and Local Government at the John F. Kennedy School of Government. This program was for about seventy elected officials and high-level managers from all over the world to attend the three-week residential seminar. I know a number of people in New Mexico who have attended these programs, including Lawrence Rael, who has held a number of high-level administrative positions in New Mexico, and was a classmate of mine that summer.

The case study method was used to help us learn how to analyze problems. The Harvard professors guided the participants through the classes, and they helped us realize that many issues had no correct or single answer. They taught us to look at all of the options and consequences, and come up with possible solutions. I brought back to New Mexico new approaches to problem solving, additional knowledge, and a network of professionals around the country. The program was worthwhile, and it helped put a new framework on policy development. It also emphasized the professional responsibilities for the inter-actions between the elected officials and the staff that implement the policies.

CHAPTER ELEVEN

Antiterrorism and Energy Legislation

Yesterday I dared to struggle. Today I dare to win.
—Bernadette Devlin

The Antiterrorism Act, HB 117, was passed in 1990, after a lot of amendments and objections from the National Rifle Association and the
numerous committees that considered the bill. I had a lot of help from
groups such as the Federal Bureau of Investigation, the state police, and the
Anti-Defamation League.

This issue was presented to me by the Anti-Defamation League as a problem in New Mexico and other rural states. Small paramilitary and antigovernment groups, such as the skinheads and Aryan Nations, were locating in rural
areas, on public land in forests hidden away in the mountains and valleys of
Montana, Idaho, Utah, Nevada, and New Mexico. The law enforcement agencies were beginning to encounter them and needed some methods to deal
with them.

The definitions section of the act was difficult, as we were dealing with
guns and weapons relating to civil disorder. Any planned act of violence by an
assemblage of two or more persons with the intent to cause damage or injury
to another individual or his property was the definition of civil disorder.

The penalty for conviction of a civil disorder is a fourth degree felony, and
the person shall be sentenced under the provisions of the Criminal Sentencing
Act to imprisonment for a definite term of eighteen months or, in the discre-
tion of the sentencing court, to a fine of not more than five thousand dollars,
or both.

This legislation was introduced three times before it passed and was signed
by the governor in 1990. The purpose was clear, but how to draft the legislation

without having problems with the National Rifle Association; the Second Amendment of the United States Constitution; and the sportsmen, hunters, and the conservationists was difficult. The first time I carried this bill in 1989 I had help from two lawyers doing pro bono work with the Anti-Defamation League, Bob Strumor and Jerry Wertheim. We went from one committee to the next in the House and got it to the floor of the House. It was on the agenda for final passage in the House, and I thought we had done our work and it would pass, but there were letters on everyone's desk from the National Rifle Association recommending they vote against the bill. The bill did not pass and we tried again the next year.

We had more amendments and more exemptions. The reason for the legislation had become more important as we had evidence of some anti-government groups locating in New Mexico. There were newspaper articles about the Aryan Nations groups in Coeur d'Alene, Idaho, and other states beginning to take action. Governor Carruthers contacted me and indicated he would sign it, as he realized it would be necessary to combat these kinds of groups.

The National Conference of State Legislatures was recommending action against these hate and antigovernment groups at our last Executive Committee meeting. We passed a resolution in 1989 that I had prepared and urged the group to pass. The resolution was presented to the annual meeting for the National Conference in June and it passed, representing the seventy-five hundred legislators in the country.

After September 11, 2001, and the attacks in New York by the Al Qaeda terrorists, the country had an added definition of terrorism. It was no longer just internal hate groups but external groups wanting to destroy the United States. This legislation was amended to include the new threat.

Energy policy has been an interest of mine for many years. It includes the depletion of oil and gas in our country, the price of energy for the consumers, alternative energy, and conservation of energy. President Jimmy Carter created the Department of Energy and did a good job of educating the public about these issues through conservation requirements for building, stockpiling oil reserves for an emergency, and pointing to an alternative energy future. The next president, Ronald Reagan, did not pursue these policies and the effort collapsed. It is now over thirty years later and President Obama is beginning to talk about a new economy using energy alternatives. The serious consequences of global climate change for our world have made it imperative that we act now to make changes.

The following excerpts are from an article I wrote with my son Todd Eisenstadt for the *Albuquerque Journal* on January 16, 1991.

IT'S TIME FOR THE UNITED STATES TO FORMULATE ENERGY POLICY

As the entire world awaits Saddam Hussein's next move, it would be easy for us all to feel overwhelmed that an irrational despot so far from our daily lives can potentially play such a deadly role. However ill-suited we at home may be to judge foreign policy decisions, there is something New Mexicans can do if we have the energy.

The crisis in the Persian Gulf will be resolved, by negotiation or by warfare. If war comes, many of our 460,000 men and women in the Saudi desert will bleed as a result of the United States' failure, since the Carter administration, to implement a coherent and comprehensive energy policy and the aggressive opportunism of Saddam Hussein.

Oil supplies to this country were disrupted in the 1970's. Then we only paid higher prices, not blood, to satisfy our gluttonous energy appetite. Is the present situation déjà vu?

As long as we rely on an inherently unstable region of the world to sate our voracious energy appetite, the Persian Gulf scenario and the energy shortages of the 1970's will play themselves out over and over.

There are solutions which a responsible federal government must adopt, and there may be ways citizens at the grassroots level can spur Washington to action. The nation was on the path to energy independence under the guidance of Jimmy Carter, who stressed conservation and the development of alternative energy sources as a substitute for the Persian Gulf oil.

Worldwide energy consumption dropped enough to break the OPEC cartel. Once that happened and the price of Middle East oil fell, the Reagan administration lacked the fortitude to stay the course.

"We wouldn't have needed any oil from the Persian Gulf after 1985 if we'd simply kept on saving oil at the rate we did from 1977 through 1985," wrote physicist and conservation advocate Amory Lovins, in a recent *New York Times* op-ed piece.

We are indeed far from the shifting sands of Saudi Arabia and should probably leave foreign policy to the diplomats. But viewing the national will as an aggregation of the wills of each state, we can take a first step towards restoring energy issues to the top of the federal agenda, and do our part at the state and local levels to reduce the country's dependence on foreign oil.

The New Mexico Legislature will consider measures that would:

A. Encourage state purchasers to consider energy conservation as well as short-term cost when buying state equipment.

B. Offer incentives for consumers to purchase fuel-efficient cars, solar tax credits, solar equipment and mandate recycling programs in all the state's urban areas.

C. Establish an energy conservation task force, to include representatives of the Los Alamos and Sandia national laboratories which, during more prosperous times, pioneered the national search for alternative energy sources.

These measures are not an end in themselves, but rather, it is hoped, the sounding of a voice that has been silent for far too long.

The time is now for New Mexicans and all Americans from our other 49 states to unite and send a message to Congress and the president that there is a strong will in this country to formulate a coherent and comprehensive energy policy, which has been absent for a decade.

Four bills I introduced during the 1991 session, House bills 267 through 270 reflected the issues discussed in the article quoted above. Representative Gary King was my prime cosponsor, and we held a press conference in the rotunda of the capitol during the session. The bills were called the Energy Conservation Task Force, Solar Energy Tax Credit, Gas Efficiency, and Life Cycle Costing acts, and we began presenting our testimony and explaining the need for these measures regarding state energy policies.

Well, just imagine the scene when we began presenting our small efforts to move toward a more efficient use of energy before the House Energy and Natural Resources Committee. There was not a seat in the room, it was standing room only and there were crowds in the hallway also. New Mexico has always been considered an oil and gas producing state, and because of the severance tax money these industries provide for the state general fund, their influence on state government has been huge.

The lobbyists were earning their money and working overtime to make sure that our bills didn't pass because they did not want any changes to the way we had always done business in New Mexico. They seemed to think that if we began a conservation program it would have dire consequences to their industry and their price for oil and gas. There would be a long period of transition before that would happen. We needed the state to begin to explore the inevitable need to protect the consumers from the runaway cost of oil and gas.

Sometimes it is necessary to introduce legislation even when the outcome can be predicted. We lost those bills, but we presented the issues and some seeds were planted.

Twenty years later on January 25, 2010, the *Albuquerque Journal* carried an advertisement from the Greater Albuquerque Chamber of Commerce describing a five-part luncheon series to focus on critical energy issues facing the state of New Mexico. Among the topics were renewable energy, solar industry, traditional sources of energy, and oil and gas.

Many of us were ahead of our time on these issues, but now I think the time has come. Now the Obama administration is proposing to get the country back on track toward an alternative energy future.

CHAPTER TWELVE

Death Threats, the State Cookie, and an Automobile Accident

The trick is what one emphasizes. We either make
ourselves miserable or we make ourselves strong.
The amount of work is the same.

—Carlos Castaneda

I received two death threats, one when I was in the House and one in the Senate. They were in response to legislation I had introduced, and the one in the House stunned me because it was a memorial I had introduced from an interim committee in 1990. The memorial was called the Children's Rights Memorial, and it was modeled after a United Nations resolution stating that children have the right to health, safety, education, and general welfare. This memorial was quite generic and an accepted idea about how to treat children in the twentieth century, at least for most people. I got an unsigned letter in the mail in which the correspondent wrote, "You have no right to tell me what to do with my children or how to raise them, they are my children. You had better watch out for yourself as I'm gunning for you and your children." At first I thought it was a crank and I was going to ignore it, but then I thought about my children at home and went to get some advice about what to do about this peculiar person's threat to my life. I was told to report this to the capitol police, which I did. I had no further incident from this threat, but I did watch my back when I went to the basement parking garage late at night. Since I'm all of five foot two I'm not sure that there was much I could do about an attack anyway.

The second death threat came in relationship to Senate Bill 155, the teaching of evolution. This bill, which I will discuss in depth later, was one paragraph that required the state board of education to adopt the National Academy of Science standards for the teaching of biology, space science, and earth science.

The bill was introduced to counter the effort to teach creationism in biology and remove evolution. It is an old argument that still hasn't gone away.

My secretary in the Senate office said that she received death threats against me, and they said, "The Evolution Bill will kill God." This threat I took very seriously and the capitol police were also quite concerned because there were large crowds of people at each committee where I testified on behalf of this bill. The police began escorting me from my office to the committee hearings and waited outside the room. The Christian Coalition had a presence in the capitol for the first time that I could remember and were lobbying against this bill. This threat was real and because of the very strong feelings it evoked I knew I needed protection. There were death threats, anonymous letters, and nasty phone calls. I'm anxious to see a movie that has been made about Charles Darwin and his life, because his discovery of the theory of evolution seems to have isolated him from his world in the 1800s.

My husband always told me that "if you can't do what you think is right then you shouldn't be there." This was an issue that I continue to believe is very important and correct scientifically, and it was the right thing for me to do in my position as a state senator. I didn't expect it to be so difficult.

On a lighter note, a bill to adopt the *bizcochito* as the state cookie was introduced in 1989. Immediately there was an amendment introduced by one of my Republican friends, Representative Don Silva, that changed the definition of the bizcochito from a small anise-flavored cookie that was brought to New Mexico by the early Spaniards to something quite different. When I went to the floor of the House that morning, there were a lot of smiles around me, and I found out the reason was that the amendment in Don's bill said "the state cookie shall be the lady from Sandoval County." Since I was the only lady from Sandoval County, I was almost the state cookie of the state of New Mexico. The sponsor of this legislation was not happy and he immediately moved a do not pass vote on the amendment. The amendment failed to pass, but not unanimously. I still laugh at this antic and enjoy remembering that for two days I was a bizcochito.

The automobile accident was something that happened to my car while it was parked in my private spot in the basement of the capitol, during my first session in the House of Representatives. I was often attending late night meetings, as a member of the House Appropriations Committee and left to get my car later than other members did.

All the members of the legislature have assigned parking places during the legislative sessions so that they can attend meetings and come and go more easily. My spot was the same as my House District number 44; that was useful, and we all remembered our locations with ease.

That particular night, toward the end of the session, I was late getting to my car in the basement. No one was driving it but me, and as I went to the assigned spot, carrying my briefcase and filled with my fatigue from a long day, I took out my key and reached for the door. It had been smashed. I couldn't understand what had happened because it was parked into the wall and then I noticed a small business card on the windshield. The space next to me was reserved for a Republican legislator from the southeast part of our state and the card was from one of his friends, also a legislator. The card said to contact the legislator whose pickup truck had smashed my car from the space next to mine.

My options were limited to three. First was to contact the capitol police and file a report. I was new in the Roundhouse and figured I didn't need a pickup truck full of Republican enemies during my first session. Second, I thought I could go to the Democrat leadership for help in arranging for the insurance companies to take care of this mess. The third option was to deal with it myself. After all I was a big girl, and I could handle this without causing a lot of fuss. I chose the third option, and I went to visit the identified representative on the floor of the House the next day. He admitted he was at fault and his insurance company would contact me. He did not apologize for the problem it would be for me, as I would need a rental car for a couple of weeks during the repair. His insurance company did not contact me immediately; I had to call him a few more times to accomplish the task.

He behaved badly after damaging my car, and I wonder if I should have chosen option one and filed a report describing his negligence. But I have learned that it was not something I wanted to be bothered with, as I wanted to devote my time and attention to other issues. The auto accident that occurred late one night in the basement of the capitol has remained unknown until now, as you read about it.

The stories of the happenings in the Roundhouse are a few that remain in my memory, and I chose them because they all illustrate what goes on during our days and nights, while we are busy making laws for the state and the people. The death threats were the most serious, and I wish they didn't occur, but perhaps it is part of the job. The state cookie is a small illustration of some of the humor that is necessary during the tension and efforts to compromise and agree about the larger issues.

The auto accident describes what happens when you put 112 people together that don't know each other, from different parts of the state, different cultures, different parties, and different ideologies about government. Put us all in a bag and shake us up and we have a legislative session. If we are lucky, we make a lot of friends from all over the state that we can enjoy, and we learn to ignore the unimportant things and continue to get the job done.

CHAPTER THIRTEEN

Ethics Legislation

It's hard to beat a person who never gives up.
—Babe Ruth

I n ethical terms, values are statements of worth or preferences that influence our thinking when we need to make choices. Our values express what we really care about in relationship to our lives as human beings. To assure that our values affect our society appropriately, we join with others to develop rules of behavior to activate those values. The prevailing values and morals held by its people represent the ethical system of a community. The term *ethics*, therefore, describes a shared system of values and morals commonly held by a group.

When I was elected to hold public office, I felt it was an honor and a public trust, and I needed to behave in a way that utilized the highest standards of ethical conduct. It was a great disappointment to me when I learned that not all of my colleagues in the legislature behaved that way, although the great majority did.

Citizens in my district, colleagues, and lobbyists began to share stories of what had happened to them during the legislative process. Lobbyists told me that a committee chairman told them that "if they wanted their bills to be heard the next day they would have to make a campaign contribution tonight." I suggested that I would go with them immediately to the Speaker's office and report this offence. But they would not do it because they felt their effectiveness as a lobbyist would be diminished. When contributions were made during the session, there were always rumors of votes for rent or for sale. There were a number of legislators that did not agree with these activities, and we began to talk about remedies such as an ethics commission.

The first of three legislative bills that I introduced and cosponsored with about three-fourths of the membership of the House was in 1990. My primary cosponsor was Representative Don Silva, a Republican with whom I shared a radio show, which I will talk about later. Our bill for ethics legislation was linked with legislative pay for New Mexico legislators. At that time, we were one of four legislative bodies in the United States that were not paid. In the first committee these two bills were separated and the constitutional amendment for legislative pay went forward while the ethics legislation was tabled in committee.

Quoting from the *Albuquerque Journal*, February 13, 1990, "Representatives Pauline Eisenstadt D-Corrales, and Don Silva R-Albuquerque, had been pushing a bill this session that would establish an ethics committee and raise legislators' salaries. While bills that would raise salaries and extend the length of sessions have been making some progress through committees, the ethics proposal had stalled."

In an attempt to push the issue, Representative Silva and I asked the House Rules Committee for a rule change that would have set up an ethics review procedure just for House members. "This was our fall back position if we thought the bill wasn't going to make it," Silva told the committee.

Committee members weren't receptive to the rule change. Several complained that any ethics rules should apply to the Senate as well as the House, and many also wondered how part-time legislators could possibly avoid conflicts of interest. According to a quote from the *Albuquerque Journal*,

> House Speaker Raymond Sanchez (D-Albuquerque) contended, "You're going to set up a situation where legislators could only be individuals who have never had to work for a living, who have no visible means of support."
>
> While critics argued that it would be very difficult to keep legislators from voting for every issue that may affect their pocketbooks, Eisenstadt pointed out that thirty-two states have managed to come up with some type of procedure to review legislator's ethics.

Others felt that the efforts in other states to curb official malfeasance didn't matter. "I don't necessarily feel, because other states have done something, it is good for New Mexico," the *Journal* quoted Representative Michael Olguin, D-Socorro. "I don't see any groundswell of support for a code of ethics for legislators." The House Rules Committee voted against establishing a House Committee to review its members' activities and requested that the Legislative Council set up an interim committee to draft an ethics code for House members.

Around the same time, on December 24, 1991, Representative Ronald Olguin of Albuquerque was charged by the attorney general with four felonies, including attempted bribery, for allegedly offering to win new state funds for a nonprofit agency if the organization would pay him fifteen thousand dollars.

Often a crisis provides an opportunity for actions that would not otherwise be possible. I introduced my second Legislative Ethics Act in January

1991. Although my friend Representative Don Silva, R-Albuquerque, had retired by then, I managed to find a very large number of cosponsors, and we tried again to restore the public's approval rating in the legislature. The University of New Mexico's Public Interest Research Group said that approval ratings had dropped to an all-time low of 26 percent. The public was interested in our passing this legislation, and it seemed that the Olguin situation demonstrated the need. But the bill received three committee referrals, and that is usually a death knell for passage during the session.

This bill created a Legislative Ethics Commission and decided how the members were selected and by whom, from both the House and the Senate. It also provided for an executive director and a small budget. Penalties for legislators, including censure, expulsion, or a letter of reprimand, and the subpoena power to call witnesses were included in the legislation.

On Saturday, March 2, 1991, the House adopted penalty provisions for the new House Ethics rule. The House rule, for the most part, reiterates existing laws against conflicts of interest and bribery. It was something of a legislative landmark and was the first such ethics rule to be adopted by either the House or the Senate. The ethics rule advises members on how to avoid conflicts of interest and using their offices for personal gain. The *Albuquerque Journal* quoted House Speaker Raymond Sanchez, D-Albuquerque, as saying that the "people have been telling us that the public perception of the legislature is low because we don't have an ethics rule. Now, we have a rule. Let's see how much credit the public and the media give us."

Sanchez said he pushed the rule only because of the public perception, not because of any evidence of rampant unethical conduct by state lawmakers. "I don't think there is anything wrong with the legislature," he said.

In the same article,

> Rep. Pauline Eisenstadt-Corrales, who has pushed ethics legislation in previous years, this year proposed an ethics statute for both the House and Senate that is much more comprehensive and stringent, than the House rule. She said Saturday she would prefer putting standards and penalties on legislative ethics into law, but called the new rule "certainly a step forward." She said adoption of the rule probably means statutory treatment for legislative ethics won't succeed this year. She said she will probably leave her more comprehensive measure on the table.

An editorial in the *Albuquerque Tribune* on March 1, 1991, reported that

> House members' easy adoption last week of rules to enforce their recently approved ethics code carried a speedy side effect—the quieting of a critic of Speaker Sanchez. Rep. Pauline Eisenstadt, a Corrales Democrat who has had past clashes with Sanchez on her ethics bill and his future as

the chamber's leader, said she is satisfied with the new rules. Sure, they don't allow for recommendations of expulsion and they don't affect the Senate, but Eisenstadt said, "They're a step forward and I'm pleased this has occurred."

"I'm laying down my sword," she declared, then paused before adding, "for now."

Even though I had hope for stronger legislation to address the problem of ethical accountability for legislators, I thought the new rule was a step forward. But I would continue to fight for more comprehensive and stringent ethics rules for both the House and Senate.

Because the composition of the ethics commission is always challenged and the citizen legislature creates problems for conflict of interest issues, ethics legislation is very difficult to pass with a majority vote. I tried one more time in a different way in 1992 with a constitutional resolution that would enable the public to vote on the creation of an ethics commission. The leadership in the House was not interested in pursuing this, and it also did not pass, although some piecemeal legislation did pass. Proposals to prohibit political fundraising by legislators during legislative sessions passed, and disclosure requirements for campaign finance and restricting personal use of unexpended campaign funds passed.

Incremental changes are the time-tested way of making reforms in legislative bodies. Because they don't know how it will work and they are more comfortable with smaller steps, legislators find big reforms like an ethics commission too threatening.

In 2010, twenty years after my legislative efforts, there were five proposals for the creation of an ethics commission in the New Mexico legislature: two in the House and three in the Senate. The arguments against the bills were similar to the ones I tried to deal with in my bills. The membership of the commission is always an issue, as are the penalties, the use of subpoena power, and transparency of the proceedings. The need is apparent, and I'm certain one day there will be an ethics commission for the legislature of the state of New Mexico.

The Representative Ron Olguin Story

In December 1991, Attorney General Tom Udall, who is now a U.S. senator, charged Representative Ron Olguin, an Albuquerque Democrat, with attempted bribery, conspiracy, and attempted fraud for promising to get Staying Straight Community Corrections, a criminal-offender counseling service, a $100,000 grant from the state, in return for a $15,000 fee. This was reported in the *Albuquerque Tribune* on December 24, 1991.

⊘ Pauline with Congressman Tom Udall (presently Senator Tom Udall), a long-time friend, in Corrales for the burial of a time capsule.

It is ironic that I had been introducing ethics legislation for two years, and then I had a small role in the development in this case against a fellow legislator. In an article from the *Albuquerque Tribune* of December 24, 1991, Udall said, "Eisenstadt played a role in the development of the attorney general's case against Olguin and should be praised for her courageous action."

The development of this situation was very awkward for me as Representative Olguin's actions were an embarrassment for the legislative body, but many of my colleagues told me I did the right thing in reporting it to the attorney general's office. I received a number of letters from my district and letters to the newspaper for my role in recommending that the group contact the attorney general. One letter from a constituent said, "Regarding Olguin, thank God for you and Wayne Maes. I only wish there were more Paulines in the legislature. Thanks to your integrity and good sense, perhaps there will be. Thanks from all in our family."

My role in this situation was minimal, but it required making a choice about what action to take or not take. On October 16, 1991, a constituent and friend called me to discuss an incident that had occurred at Conflict Management Inc. (CMI). Dr. Wayne Maes was the clinical director of CMI, which provides counseling and therapy.

Dr. Maes described a situation involving a state legislator, whose identity Dr. Maes did not know, who had solicited money from CMI to help them, by exerting political influence to boost the level of state funding received for a community corrections program. His associates at CMI felt that this behavior represented a potential conflict of interest, unethical behavior, and possible illegal behavior. Dr. Maes requested my recommendations.

I recommended that the attorney general be called to judge whether a further investigation was warranted. We decided that I would contact the attorney general to make him aware of the situation. AG Tom Udall said that he needed to know more about the allegations, as they could, if true, represent illegal activity. I gave him Dr. Maes's phone number, and I heard nothing more until December 19, 1991. Tom Udall called me to notify me that as a result of the ensuing investigation, there was a criminal case against Representative Ron Olguin and charges would be filed shortly.

With this pending, I called to let Speaker Raymond Sanchez know what I knew. He said, "You've been telling us about ethical problems for three years and I guess you were right. The system worked well—the criminal was caught—everything worked as it was supposed to. We don't need any new laws."

I then called Governor Bruce King to alert him to the AG's forthcoming charges against Representative Ron Olguin. He thanked me and expressed his sorrow, as we both knew when a public official is charged for wrongdoing it makes us all look bad.

The case proceeded in the courts, and Representative Ron Olguin and another man were found guilty the next year. Tom Udall and I continued to call for ethics reform, but we did not have the support of the leadership. In the House my last bill had over half of the member's signatures but it did not get through the committee process.

In the fall of 1992 I was one of the recipients of the Governor's Award for Outstanding New Mexico Women. I remember going to the front of the

✪ A banquet honoring "Outstanding New Mexico Women" 1992: Loretta Armenta, chairwoman of the Commission on the Status of Women; Alice King, Governor Bruce King; and Pauline.

room to talk with the governor and Alice King to receive my award. I mentioned to Bruce that it was ironic that I was receiving an award that night and Representative Olguin had been convicted and might go to jail that same week. Governor King bent down and patted me on the back and said, "Pauline, we all get what we deserve."

CHAPTER FOURTEEN

At Home from 1993 to 1996

I shall be telling this with a sigh
Somewhere ages and ages hence:
Two roads diverged in a wood, and I—I took the one less traveled by,
And that has made all the difference.

—Robert Frost, originally appeared in
The Poetry of Robert Frost edited by Edward Connery Lathem.
Henry Holt and Company, New York

After eight years in the New Mexico House of Representatives it was time to reevaluate my options, politically and personally. I needed the time to think about my family commitments, the direction of my future career, my major interests, and what my next challenges would be in the future.

President Bill Clinton had been elected in 1993, and many of us had worked hard to get him a majority of the votes in New Mexico. It was very close. We were invited to the inauguration and the invitation was impressive. "The Presidential Inaugural Committee requests the honor of your presence to attend and participate in the Inauguration of William Jefferson Clinton as president of the United States of America and Albert Gore Jr. as vice president of the United States of America on Wednesday, the twentieth of January one thousand nine hundred and ninety-three in the City of Washington."

I have kept the invitation and look at it today with regret that we were unable to attend. "The commemorative Invitation Celebrates our nation's Fifty-Second Presidential Inauguration. Americans join together to witness their president take a simple thirty-five word oath of office and witness the triumph of representative democracy through the peaceful transfer of political power according to the will of the people." It still gives me goose bumps to realize what our country has brought to the world in the form of a democratic form of government. As a footnote, it was stated at the bottom of the page that for the first time in history the entire Presidential Inaugural Invitation Package is

⚙ Congressman Bill Richardson, later Governor Richardson, with Pauline at a political rally in Albuquerque Civic Plaza.

engraved and printed on recycled paper. I'm sure that was something that Al Gore added, as he is quite an environmentalist and I wish he had succeeded when he ran for president.

One spring afternoon in 1993, I got a phone call from my congressman, Bill Richardson. He asked what I was doing the next day and I replied, "Nothing in particular. What would you like me to do?" He said, "I want you to stay by your phone as I'm going to be appointed secretary of the interior and I want you to run for my seat and I will support you." That would have been perfect timing for me, as I had been thinking about running for Congress. Well, I waited by the phone but the news was not good, as Governor Bruce Babbitt of Arizona was appointed secretary of interior. Bill Richardson was appointed about two years later as ambassador to the United Nations, but by then I was already committed to running for the state Senate.

Whenever a new president is elected, or even a new governor, people begin to speculate about who will be appointed to positions in the new administration. The speculation began with the Clinton administration, and my name was mentioned repeatedly for a position in the Department of Energy dealing with alternative and renewable energy.

I talked with my old friends in Washington involved in these areas of the Department of Energy and they were very supportive. I was nominated for a position as assistant secretary of energy for renewable and alternative energy.

✪ Pauline and Mel, grand marshals for the Corrales July 4 parade.

✪ Trip to Spain with Mel.

✪ Fishing in Costa Rica with our sons, Todd and Keith.
We ate the fish Todd caught for two days.

I was in Washington for meetings, and I met with Congressman Richardson about this position. He was very supportive. I was meeting with him in the House lounge when he called the secretary of energy, Hazel O'Leary, to speak on my behalf.

This was a job I was willing to take, and I worked hard to get it by requesting that people who knew Hazel send her letters of recommendation for me. I knew Hazel from my early days as chairwoman of the Department of Energy Consumer Advisory Committee, where she served as staff director. I met with her assistant in Washington and gave her a notebook of letters recommending me for the position. About two weeks later I received an invitation to fly to Washington and meet with Hazel about the job. I knew she would be in Albuquerque the following week and I suggested we meet in Albuquerque and save the airfare and hotel money, which they were going to pay.

We met in Albuquerque; the meeting was cordial and friendly but not productive for me. I did not get the job offer. That was a road not taken, and it was probably for the best as I went on to serve in the state Senate and had a career in New Mexico, which enabled me to make a difference in people's lives.

Congressman Richardson became Ambassador Richardson, Secretary of Energy Richardson, and then Governor Richardson of New Mexico. Bill was an outstanding congressman, a good secretary of energy, a well-regarded ambassador to the United Nations, and a visionary governor. His administration put the Rail Runner train in place from Belen to Santa Fe; established the Spaceport, which will enable space tourism for the future; enlarged the film industry's presence in New Mexico; helped develop the technology sector of business in our state; and provided more money for school teachers and new infrastructure projects.

Governor Richardson ran for the presidential nomination in 2008. We supported him. Although he lost the prize, he helped put New Mexico on the American stage. His final term has expired, and there is a lot of speculation about his next "road taken." I believe he has been an effective governor and a leader who has carried New Mexico to the next level of our state's accomplishments. I retired in 2000 from the state Senate and did not have the opportunity to serve with him during his administration.

A number of activities that I had neglected during my time in the House of Representatives were now on my schedule again. One of these was playing tournament tennis. When we lived in Puerto Rico, I started to play a lot of tennis, and it was a sport that I really enjoyed. I played singles with my friend Fredita Frontera. She almost always beat me in the game, but I learned a lot from her.

In 1993, my husband and I played at the Rio Rancho Country Club. By then I was playing mixed and ladies doubles. I was asked to join the Ladies Fifty and Over doubles league tennis team for Rio Rancho. Our team won the

☀ Tennis champs—the Rio Rancho ITAS Senior Women's tennis team recently won the Northern New Mexico District title with a 3-2 record. Left to right: Mikki Roth, Pat Bodwell, Audrey Stern, Fran Keck, Pauline, and Pat Scimonelli. We went to the district tournament in Phoenix, Arizona, but we lost.

Albuquerque fifty and over doubles league tennis championship. I was not at the top of our team's ability, but somewhere in the middle and I got pulled along into the 1995 sectional finals in Phoenix, Arizona.

I mention this because I think there are connections between sports and politics.

Competition is a big part of the game of politics, wanting to win, watching for your move, anticipating the opposition, and hitting the sweet spot for victory in tennis or passing legislation. The need to work with teammates is critical; passing the ball if the shot is better for them, and covering the back of the court, not always in the front. These are useful in politics and life.

The Rio Rancho Rotary Club became an active part of my life. I worked first on the International Committee chairing an exchange with the town of Zacatecas, Mexico. The Zacatecas club in Mexico stated that they needed a garbage truck that would compact their city's garbage. They were presently jumping up and down on the garbage to compact it for their city. One of our members was the manager of Waste Management for the state of New Mexico. He indicated that they were going to replace one of their compacter trucks, and he could donate it to Mexico and get the tax benefits.

✪ Visit with my mother Anne and sister Mickey.

This was a very exciting event for the Zacatecans and for our Rotary Club in Rio Rancho. Two car loads of Mexican Rotarians drove for two days to come to Rio Rancho to receive the documents for the garbage truck for their town. We had activities for them, and Channel 4 came to Rio Rancho to film the ceremony. It was a happy time for all of us, and I can still envision the trucks with the men jumping up and down to compact the garbage.

After this activity, I was selected to be president of the Rio Rancho Rotary Club for 1995–1996. The Rotary Club continues to be a part of my life and activities as it provides service to the community as well as international service. Service is an important ingredient in my life, and I particularly enjoy working with Rotarians because they are an international group with goals and accomplishments all around the world.

The Anti-Defamation League is a community group that I have worked with for more than twenty years, as a board member and state chairwoman from 1994 to 1995. The ADL is a formidable organization that confronts prejudice against minorities, including religious minorities such as Jewish people, hate crimes against homosexuals, Hispanics (particularly immigrants), and African Americans. They have a three-pronged approach of investigating, educating, and protecting in their work.

ADL monitors and tracks the efforts of hate-mongering extremists and their groups as well as domestic terrorists. They publish their findings and

○ The Nile River trip with Mel in Luxor, Egypt.

○ I rode that camel around the pyramids in Cairo, Egypt, but I was not his leader.

distribute them globally to teachers, elected officials, law enforcement, media, and community leaders. ADL works hard to break down stereotypes and combat bias before it becomes a source of hatred and violence. They also assist victims of hate and bigotry across all races and religions and work to expose and combat purveyors of hatred in our midst, and in cyberspace.

Susan Seligman, the executive director for New Mexico, has been a steady force in our state to prevent outbreaks of these kinds of issues and curtail them when they occur. Her leadership has been recognized throughout the community and nationally.

The Café Broads

A group of interesting woman began meeting informally; no agenda, just to talk about politics, lives, humor, and helping each other when possible. I was asked to join in the spring of 1994, and I really enjoyed the diversity of the group and the easy camaraderie of the women. We had met at various restaurants, but finally settled on the Broadway Café near downtown and hence we became the Café Broads.

The women were involved in politics, government employees, university employees, media people, a judge, a hospital employee, and some business types. All of the women were in management positions. The informal leadership of the group consisted of scheduling the meetings and alerting everyone about the time and place. Linda Valencia Martinez was our leader during the year and a half that I was able to attend.

We laughed, shared gossip, stories, and opinions about anything and everything. We made new friends and had a special network. I think it is important for women working in male-dominated fields to have other women to associate with and help each other with similar problems. When I declared my intention to run for the state Senate, I had immediate support from the group and one of them, Diane Denish, hosted a fundraising party for me when I was campaigning for that office.

CHAPTER FIFTEEN

The Media
Communicating with the Public

Far and away the best prize that life has to offer is
the chance to work hard at work worth doing.
—Theodore Roosevelt

The media in all of its forms has been an integral part of my public career.
Many politicians shun the media as they believe the media distorts what
they say, or that they are looking for the negatives in the story. My experience with the media has been very positive, and I believe the importance of
the media cannot be overstated.

Newspapers

My political career spanned the 1980s and 1990s, when newspapers were very
prominent in the public arena. It was important to have two major newspapers in Albuquerque, as they had different points of view, different editorial policies, and they kept each other honest. Many of us felt sad when the
Albuquerque Tribune closed its press in 2008. Jack Ehn, the editorial page editor of the *Tribune*, always found the human side of the story. Kate Nelson was
the Santa Fe reporter for the *Tribune* back when I was going from one committee to another with my ethics legislation. She came with me on that journey, and she understood what I was trying to accomplish. Ollie Reed wrote
great stories about real people that left a lasting impression. The editors that I
remember, John Temple and Tim Gallagher, got out into the community and
had an impact.

Some of the *Journal* reporters that worked the political beat were John
Robertson, who always did his homework; John Yeager, who now works for
the Legislative Council Service; and Loie Fecteau. Both Yeager and Fecteau
were effective reporters. Jim Belshaw was always one of my favorite columnists

because he always wrote about people through a different-colored lens and could see things in a situation that the rest of us missed. Bill Hume was the editorial page editor, and I always read what he wrote carefully. Jerry Crawford was the editor and Kent Walz was an assistant editor during that time period. We knew Kent Walz, who is now the editor of the *Albuquerque Journal*, as my husband and Kent were in the same law school class at the University of New Mexico. We always joke about being related through our dogs, as he came to get one of our puppies for his children. His children paged for me when I was in the Senate, brought to Santa Fe by Kent's mom, who was a constituent of mine in Cedar Crest.

The smaller newspapers were important in all of my local communities, and I subscribed to all of them and they helped me keep up with what was happening in their local areas. The *Corrales Comment*, published by Jeff Radford, enables our little community to stay involved with all of the activities and needs of this community. The *Rio Rancho Observer* during those years was published by Mike and Genie Ryan. They got involved in the community and provided some cohesion for the community. The *East Mountain Telegraph*, edited by Geri Ostrow, provided the glue for the little communities in the East Mountain areas. Placitas also had a newspaper, and there was one for Sandoval County. They helped to keep people informed.

After each session, I tried to write about what went on and send it to these community papers to inform the public about what happened in the session and what I may have accomplished for the communities. I called these articles "Legislative Reports," or "District 44 Reports," or "Capitol Comment Reports." The *Corrales Comment* and the *Rio Rancho Observer* would print them, as well as some of the smaller papers, and I always had a good response from the public.

The "Capitol Government Reports," edited by Jack Flynn, was a one-page newsletter distributed in the capitol once or twice a week. It was an insider gossip sheet with bits of information about legislation and political maneuvering between legislators and the administration on key issues. I have one paper in my files from 1990 that talked about the Workers' Compensation Bill. Jack also talked about the potential House leadership fight for Speaker, as Representative Toby Michael had announced that he was challenging Representative Raymond Sanchez. I noticed that the legislative staff as well as the legislators read this little newsletter. Mr. Flynn seemed to have the respect of the people in the political arena, but I never understood who was funding this bit of news and gossip. It was delivered free and we all read it. This newsletter was no longer available when I returned to the Senate in 1997.

Newspapers around the country and the world are in a period of transition as the new telecommunication systems such as the Internet, websites, Facebook, Twitter, Kindles, and other methods of sharing information have changed the marketplace of ideas. The advertising dollars are diminished for newspapers, and they are returning to focusing on local news because the national and international news is available elsewhere. In 2010 there was a lot of legislative coverage in the *Albuquerque Journal* and that has not been done for quite awhile.

Democracy requires informed participation from the electorate to function. Journalism that has been fact-checked and speaks the truth to the public is what is required for our system to flourish. I have wondered what will happen if there is no marketplace of ideas that we can all trust, read on a daily basis, and is not just for those that can afford to pay for the news. Television fills a different role and cannot replace an in-depth story of investigative reporting or analysis of policy issues. Our world is facing many changes in this time of global economies and technology shifts. But information is so important for a political system that requires knowledge to make decisions that the ability of the news media to survive is critical.

Our Corner of the Roundhouse Radio Show

In 1989 Representative Don Silva, a Republican friend, and I taped a twice weekly radio show, which was taken to Albuquerque for the 5:30 p.m. news those evenings. The time slot picked up a lot of listeners, because it was "go home" time. We had a command performance for people in their cars, and I recall that we did the show for two sessions. What a great time we had doing this radio show in my office in the Roundhouse.

The manager of KKOB radio was Art Schreiber, and he was a knowledgeable radio executive who wanted to make sure his listeners were well informed about the activities in Santa Fe during the legislative sessions. We were talking about the possibility of a radio show from Santa Fe and he liked the idea. We proceeded from there. We needed the political balance of a Democrat and a Republican, and I mentioned Representative Don Silva, as I had been working with him on the Centers of Technical Excellence legislation. Art thought Don would be terrific. He also had a nice deep voice, which was great for radio.

Art provided a tape recorder, a microphone, some tapes, and plenty of enthusiasm, and sent us on our way. We came up with the name *Our Corner of the Roundhouse*. The capitol building in Santa Fe is shaped in a circle and it is referred to as the Roundhouse. We liked the idea of putting a corner on a Roundhouse. It provided some edges to our show, we hoped.

We tried to tape in the early afternoon, twice a week, and invited guests, such as our congressman Bill Richardson, visiting dignitaries, and sponsors of legislation. In the last segment of the show, Don and I recounted what the major issues were for that day. I think we had thirty minutes, but with breaks, it became about twenty-three minutes. It was a trick to get it to the station in time, and Don took responsibility for that part of the logistics. The show provided some immediacy for the public by legislators who were involved in the action in Santa Fe. We were not confrontational with each other; instead we tried to inform the public. When we disagreed we stated so and tried to explain our positions. It took our time, but we both agreed it was worthwhile, and we received a lot of comments that indicated the public liked the show.

Television

Going through my video cassettes, many of which I've transferred to DVDs, I've looked at some of the interviews that were recorded of me in Santa Fe in the early days of my career. It was like going back in time and looking at another Pauline, with long hair, lots of excitement regarding things to be accomplished, and hope for the future. One episode in particular struck me. In 1990 KNME, our public broadcasting station, came to Santa Fe and interviewed me outside the capitol, then followed me inside to finish the interview. I had lots of ideas and still thought that we could move faster on fixing problems. I'm very pleased to have these DVDs as I'm hoping my grandchildren will watch some of them and feel the excitement of accomplishing some of their own dreams.

At Week's End was a show that was produced by Mary Kate Mendoza for KNME in 1992, narrated by Roger Morris. The show on December 18, 1992, celebrated the "Year of the Woman." It was the year when Anita Hill came forward to denounce Clarence Thomas during his Supreme Court nominating hearings for sexual harassment. It pointed out to the country and women in particular that the political system was dominated by old men. The seniority system still rules in our Congress and our state legislatures.

The hour-long show selected three women to feature for their success in their fields. I was selected as a woman of power in politics. Dr. Barbara McAneny was selected for her prominence in the health care arena, and Dr. Maria Chavez for her outstanding work in family development, particularly child development in low-income areas. I later served on Maria's board of directors for a period of time. Dr. Barbara McAneny has gone on to develop one of the outstanding cancer facilities in New Mexico. It was an honor for me to be included in this group of women.

They interviewed me as I went to a school in Corrales, a business in Rio Rancho, and at our Corrales home. As I viewed this tape again, I remember that the questions they asked me were insightful and required a thoughtful response. What made you successful in the man's world of politics? I said that tenacity and a willingness to confront the men with my issues, such as prenatal care for all women, money in the budget to deal with prevention of child abuse, and an ethics commission.

I was always willing to risk losing on my legislation because I knew that new ideas sometimes take time to change attitudes. "Women need to be more forceful and a part of the decision making," said Dr. McAneny.

They asked me what I would recommend for young women hoping to enter the political arena and I said, "Get a good education, learn how to compromise, feel passionate about your issues, and stand your ground while trying to convince others of your solutions to some of the major issues." Also, learn from others, men and women. And don't be afraid to keep trying. There are many ways to help your communities, and there are never enough hands and willing hearts to work for the benefit of all of us.

New Mexico Today and Tomorrow
Channel 7, KOAT

In the 1980s I had a TV show on Channel 13 called *Consumer Viewpoint*, which helped fulfill the media's requirement to provide public service. The show's main purpose was to interview people concerned with consumer topics. These shows appeared early on Sunday mornings and we were all volunteers, not paid to perform. I enjoyed producing and hosting these TV shows, and it gave us a chance to put the issues out on the airwaves. The public service requirement was removed when the telecommunications were deregulated and many of these kinds of shows are no longer seen, except on public broadcasting stations such as KNME Channel 5 in Albuquerque.

In 1993 I presented an idea for a show called *New Mexico Today and Tomorrow* to the manager of Channel 7, Mary Lyn Roper; she agreed with the concept of the show, so we proceeded. The purpose of the show was to discuss public affairs of the state of New Mexico such as health care, education, taxes, reapportionment, children's issues, technology changes, and many others. The shows began airing twice a month in June 1993 and continued for a year, until June 1994. I was the producer and host of most of the shows, although we did shift the host position when the expertise on the topic changed. We selected former state senator Victor Marshall, Republican, and Dr. Chris Garcia, professor of political science at the University of New Mexico, to be the additional hosts of the show.

I would select the timely topic for the week and fax it to Victor and Chris, with some background information and ask for their input. Then I would find the government or other expert to complement our discussion and invite them to come to our tapings, which occurred on Thursday evenings at 7:00 p.m. We arrived early and helped set up the seating arrangement and place for our guest. I got to know and like the station managers for the public affairs programs. Mary Decker was our first manager and Jenny Threet, daughter of our good friends Laura and Ed Threet, was our last manager. We appreciated their assistance as well as the cameramen.

In the beginning there was no set for us. We sat in folding chairs all in a row, like birds on a wire. I talked with the management and suggested someone go to Lowes and get one of those desks we could assemble, so that we would have something to put papers on and so that we could fidget with our feet, behind the desk. As the only one who wore a dress, I appreciated the chance to move my legs around, without the cameras watching. We got a desk, and then we got a big sign that said, *New Mexico Today and Tomorrow*, on the wall behind us.

We had quite a good mix of opinions on every issue. For example, on the show in July 1993 on taxes, Victor Marshall felt we should almost always cut spending rather than raise taxes, while Chris Garcia said it is hard to cut a program that benefits people. I wanted to find ways to help solve problems with child abuse, prenatal care, education, and economic development. The state had a budget deficit of about $50–$75 million, and the discussion was always between raising taxes or cutting spending. The frequent outcome is a little of both and when the deficit is huge, like in 2010, it becomes painful to make the decisions.

During the introduction to the shows, I would try to find an appropriate quote or explanation about the topic. For this show I quoted from Oliver Wendell Holmes, who said, "Taxes are the price we pay for a civilized society." Secretary of Taxation and Revenue Dick Minzner was our expert guest, and as a former state representative, he understood the political ramifications of the issue quite well.

Dick indicated that our state revenues pay for what we have now and that we have a structural deficit driven by the federal government because of Medicaid and the legal requirements for the Corrections Department. The major portion of our state budget was education, then it was about 70 percent of our budget, and I know it is less today. Victor's response to that was to say, "We will have tax increases forever or we will have to cut education." Economic development and more jobs are two ways to grow the pie and create more revenue, as well as cost savings and new efficiencies like joint purchasing for all state agencies.

Another topic we discussed was reapportionment, which happens after every census. The issues become very complicated and the term *gerrymandering* describes funny geographic districts that are drawn to accommodate legislators so they can have a winning district. Our guest was Judge Harris Hartz from the State Appeals Court, and he discussed the Supreme Court's ruling on a North Carolina district that was gerrymandered to save a member's district. This particular district was extremely long and narrow because it ran along a freeway in North Carolina. The ruling of the Supreme Court would have an effect on all of the states as it related to a prohibition against drawing districts along racial lines.

Reapportionment is the most serious change that takes place every ten years, based on the shift, growth, or loss of population. I participated in the reapportionment discussion for the 1990 census. This is an inside game for the politicians because the lines of the district they represent are changed, the congressional districts change, and everyone is tense and paying close attention. I witnessed Senate and House districts that were split up and some legislators were deliberately cut out of their own districts. Most of the effort is very difficult and performed by consultants with computers, maps, and calculators. Our consultant was Brian Sanderoff, director of Research and Polling, a private company, and he was an expert for this process.

Because he taught classes about this issue, Chris Garcia was our host for the reapportionment program. Brian Sanderoff, our legislative expert for the reapportionment, was a former student of his at the University of New Mexico. As the population has shifted, reapportionment has changed the legislature to more of an urban-dominated than a rural body. It also has done away with most of the swing districts, between Republican and Democrat, as the districts are now safe for the different parties. My House and Senate districts were always swing districts, which meant that I had to understand issues from both sides of the aisle. My districts were also always the largest districts in the state. When the average number of people in a Senate district was about forty-five thousand people, my district already had seventy-five thousand people. My House district always had as many as most Senate districts.

This was a most interesting show because we all knew a lot about the topic, academically with Chris and personally with Victor and me, as legislators. In 2010, another census was taken and the data arrived about one and a half years later. Then the fireworks begin. The governor's race is critical in this process as the governor has a veto over the plans that are drawn for all of the districts.

We all enjoyed these TV shows, and I still meet people who tell me that they watched all the time, even at 7:00 a.m. on Sunday morning. This program gave me a lot of comfort and ease in front of the camera and speaking on television, which helped me in my future career.

Capitol Crossfire in the New Mexico State Senate

Capitol Crossfire was a new format for a TV show developed by Channel 7, KOAT. In 1998 Dick Knipfing talked with me about doing this new show during my second year in the state Senate. The idea was to do a live call-in show from the public to the Roundhouse and ask questions of two legislators, from different parties, with different policy positions. I recommended Senator Billy

⊛ Pauline and Senator Billy McKibben getting ready for the TV show
Capitol Crossfire in the Santa Fe Roundhouse TV studio.

McKibben, a Republican from Hobbs, because he was smart, had a good sense
of humor, and was comfortable with the media.

KOAT sent staff and equipment to Santa Fe twice a week. Billy and I used
the television room in the Roundhouse, above the Senate chambers, to talk
with the people around the state of New Mexico. Dick Knipfing and Augusta
Meyers moderated our discussions and gave us the questions from the people
in the state, from their television station in Albuquerque.

Dick Knipfing would introduce the show this way, "Two of the most
knowledgeable people in the legislature" or "Two feisty state Senators" will
discuss the issues in Santa Fe and they will answer your questions. He would
then give a phone number. I would pick a topic for the show two days before,
discuss it with Billy, and then fax it to the station with some discussion of our
differing positions.

It put a big smile on my face to watch the DVDs of these shows a dozen
years later. We discussed a number of topics, including taxes, school vouchers,
private prisons, budget battles, the value of the legislature, and education. The
topics are similar from year to year as the major issue is to allocate resources
or revenue to education, human services and health care, state police, corrections, and other departments that help state government function and provide
the services to the citizens of New Mexico.

Billy and I disagreed on most issues, but we were not disagreeable with each other. We liked each other, but neither of us was a shrinking violet, and we argued enough that Dick Knipfing would say, "Okay, let's move on to the next question." The baseline difference between us was that I believe that government has a role to play in making life better for all of us and Billy thinks people should take responsibility for themselves. "Government takes too much money in taxes," according to Billy, "and the legislative session is a feeding frenzy for more programs." It was the frequent fault line between the Republican and Democratic parties, however we agreed around the margins on issues.

Billy was the major sponsor for a cigarette tax to be earmarked for the University of New Mexico Cancer Center, and I cosponsored that bill along with many others. I chaired the Higher Education Interim Committee and felt strongly that we should have a unified system of higher education and also that we have too many institutions of higher education in our poor state. Billy cosponsored a joint memorial with me to put a moratorium on building new institutions of higher education in the state.

Most of the questions from the public were not related to the topic we were talking about in the first segment of the show. They took the opportunity to talk about whatever they wanted to discuss, and sometimes it was an opportunity to listen to their concerns.

School vouchers was a topic that Billy and I had major differences on. The issue was to provide vouchers to students, which provided money to the private school of their choice, if the school would admit them. The money would come out of the public school budget formula. My position was that vouchers would have a negative effect on the public schools because the private schools would cherry-pick the better students and leave the public schools with the problem students.

Democracy is at risk without public schools, where young people learn and understand how to get along with each other and help each other achieve at different levels. We learn respect for our differences and create bonds with people who are not just in our same economic, religious, or intellectual levels or groups. Vouchers could not be used in forty-seven school districts, as they had no private schools in those districts. I thought that a voucher was a simplistic fix for a complex problem. Billy said that we needed competition in the public schools. He publicly referred to the NEA, the National Education Association, as the Never Enough Association.

Vouchers as a policy did not pass that year, but charter schools began as another possibility to inject competition into the public school arena. The charter schools are flourishing now, and I think they have provided more opportunities for students to attend school in smaller environments and special interests. They are funded by the public school budget, and they need a lot more oversight than they are getting now. I voted for them in 1999 and am hopeful that they will enhance the possibility of greater success for our students.

Billy and I had a good time with *Capitol Crossfire* and we became friends. We were both pragmatic enough to work together when we agreed that something was important. The Republicans were always in the minority during all of my years in the legislature and that makes it hard for them to pass legislation, if they wanted to, without help from the majority Democrats. The role for the minority becomes that of the naysayer in state legislatures and nationally in Congress. It is a difficult role as it is so negative, without friends in the opposition.

Sometime in 1999 Billy and I were attending a meeting of the Cancer Patient Support Services, where we were both recognized for our efforts on their behalf, when we stepped out to get some coffee. He told me he was considering running for governor as an Independent, and he asked if I would consider running as his lieutenant governor. I knew that he had a primary opponent in his district in Hobbs, but I didn't realize that he was ready to become an Independent. I was flattered that he asked me, but I was still willing to work with the Democrats and becoming an Independent did not seem to be a winning strategy. Whenever I have run for office, I have evaluated the numbers and the data and only run if I thought I could win. Billy did not run in 2000 for his Senate seat or for governor as an Independent. We have talked once a year since then. He spends most of his time in Texas, and I'm certain they enjoy his humor as much as we all did. He would make an outrageous statement, give you a wink, and move on.

Sometimes while we were taping *Capitol Crossfire* in the afternoon above the Senate floor, our colleagues would be on the floor debating bills. We were waiting for the television setup and looking down on the floor when Billy said, "I tell my Republicans that they only talk to each other, while Pauline and I talk to the whole state." Here's winking at you, Billy.

CHAPTER SIXTEEN

The State Senate of New Mexico
1996–2000

Never doubt that a small group of thoughtful,
committed citizens can change the world.
Indeed, it the only thing that ever has.

—Margaret Mead

Serving in the state Senate was quite different than the state House of Representatives in New Mexico, primarily because of the reduced size of the Senate. It had forty-two members compared with seventy members in the House. There was also a lighter reign by the leadership: there was more consultation, more asking for support, and more inclusion in the decision making for the members. For example, we had a sheet of paper on which we suggested the committee referrals for our bills, which we gave to the majority leader. In the House the bills were assigned to committees by the Speaker. I remember receiving three committee referrals, for all of my ethics bills. Unless there are duplicate bills in each house, the likelihood of getting a bill through both houses and all of the committees in a thirty-day session is nearly impossible, and even in a sixty-day session it is not a good bet.

My first year in the Senate I was in a first floor suite with several newcomers to the Senate, as the seniority system gives preference to the longer-term senators. We shared offices and my suite mates were senators Linda Lopez, Dede Feldman, Cisco McSorley, and Phil Maloof. We were all first termers except Phil, and he had his own office. Cisco and I were the only ones in the Senate, at that time in the Democrat caucus, that had also served in the House, and we agreed that we liked the Senate better. We also had the benefit of some relationships in the House when it came time to have our legislation heard in the House committees.

At the beginning of a legislative session there were a lot of receptions and social events that I would attend because the committees were not yet hearing

○ At my desk on the floor of the Senate.

○ Opening day of the session 1997: Todd, Mireya, me, and Mel.

bills. The procedural work of introducing bills, getting cosponsors and committee assignments was grinding. Our four suite mates would try to drive to the receptions together, and Cisco and I would help the others understand how the legislative system worked.

Our little group added Senator Richard Romero and during the first year, between sessions we would meet in an Albuquerque restaurant and discuss issues of concern to us. It was informal and I would send a note around or call to determine everyone's availability and the topic. I would also always

○ Lunch at La Fonda after the opening day of the legislature.

○ Senator Manny Aragon, president
pro tem of the New Mexico Senate.
Courtesy of the New Mexico
Legislative Council Service.

inform and invite Senator Manny Aragon to join us, if he wished. We didn't
solve the problems, but we enjoyed arguing with each other and developed
relationships with each other that were helpful during the sessions.

Senator Manny Aragon dominated the Senate after serving there for
twenty-nine years, and he was president pro tem when I was elected in 1996.
Manny Aragon was a complex man with many different sides to his personality.
He was extremely smart, compassionate, kind, with terrific sense of humor,
and sometimes a bully all wrapped inside one person. He was the kind of man

⊙ The Rio Rancho Chamber of Commerce, visiting in the Roundhouse.

⊙ My friends from the Rotary Club of Rio Rancho. I am a proud member and former president of this club.

that everyone liked, me too, but you learned to pay attention when he wanted something.

Manny came to my desk on the floor of the Senate during the first week of the session, and he had a sheet of white paper with him, which had three columns he had scratched on the paper. He said, "Pauline, I need your help with two of my projects. Would you give me $25,000 of your capital project (pork) money for either the Hispanic Cultural Center or the Balloon Fiesta

⚙ The Placitas Open Space Advocates held an ice cream party for me to celebrate success in Santa Fe.

Park?" One column on his paper was headed by the Hispanic Cultural Center and one column was headed by the Balloon Fiesta Park. I asked, "Manny, what is the column in the middle?" He said, "That is my shit list for those who don't give me anything." I started to laugh and told him that I would think about it. The projects were good and I supported them, but they were not in my district. But he was intimidating as the president of the Senate. I laughed out loud and thought he had a lot of audacity to try to take some of the money I needed for projects in my district such as roads, schools, ambulances, libraries, and community centers.

Richard Romero sat near me and I went over to him, described what had happened, and he said, "Forget it, spend the money on your district." So for a short while I was on Manny's "shit list." But that first year nobody got to spend any money for capital projects in the House or the Senate as Senator William Davis talked it to death. We were sitting on the floor of the Senate on the final day waiting to vote on the capital projects, but Senator Bill Davis held the floor and wouldn't give it up. We never had a chance to vote yes. All of the projects did not pass.

My committee assignments were on the Senate Finance Committee and the Conservation Committee. The Senate Finance Committee is a major committee that deals with the state budget and all of the legislation that is introduced that requires money. I requested this committee assignment because it is the hub of the legislative process. Sitting on the Finance Committee you learn about the

⚙ Hugs from the children of Carroll Elementary School in the town of Bernalillo.

state budget, the departments in the state that provide the service, and the revenue stream that provides for state government. The capital projects flow through the Senate Finance Committee and all of the bills that require appropriations come before the finance committees in the House and the Senate.

Having a voice and a vote on the Senate Finance Committee was an opportunity to influence legislation that I thought was beneficial for our state and people. The problem with the committee was that it was working all the time, and it was hard to get all the members present. We all had other minor committee assignments—mine was the Conservation Committee. I enjoyed that also because the rural part of our state has a lot of clashes between the farmers and ranchers and the environmental groups. There were new issues for me to learn about.

Big game hunting was a new issue for me. How many tags are permitted for each of the animals on the ranches and how many tags for the ranchers? The land is privately owned but the game is not. There is a lottery during the seasons for deer hunting, elk hunting, and turkey shooting as well fishing licenses. The applications for a tag, which is the license to hunt and kill an animal, are very valuable. One of the most hotly contested issues I witnessed was the effort to change how many tags would be issued and to whom.

We had to meet in the House chambers to accommodate the crowd when this issue was presented. The livelihood of small rural areas is connected to big game hunting, and of course, the conservationists want to preserve the game. There were a lot of people in the capitol that wanted to talk to me about their point of view, and they were often big men wearing cowboy clothes, big hats,

○ My guests, Justin Rinaldi and his granddaughters Jessica and Alexis. The girls were my pages for the day.

and big smiles. They taught me a lot about this part of our state. One of them invited me to go on a big game hunt, but I told him that I could not kill an animal, I only wanted to take pictures. He said he does those kinds of trips also.

I did not go with him, but years later my husband and I went with the state Game and Fish Department to find the bugling elks. We were up at 4:00 a.m. to go to the state preserve near Chama to listen to the bull elks calling their cows. We got close to the elks as we hid behind trees, and the guide had a whistle that sounded like the cows. I understood what importance these animals had for our state. It amused me to learn that about ten bulls could service a herd of one hundred cows. My male colleagues on the Conservation Committee enjoyed that bit of information also.

Once all of the legislative bills were assigned to committees, my days became consumed with attendance on the Senate Finance Committee, except when I was presenting my own bills in other committees. Toward the end of the session there was a big backlog, and we would meet in the morning before the floor session as well as in the afternoon. In the last weeks, we met all the time to hear the House bills.

All of the bills pile up in the Senate Finance Committee and the House Appropriations and Finance Committee at the end of the session. During my second year in the Senate I had a couple of bills sitting in the Finance Committee that I had worked very hard to prepare and present to the legislature. One of them was Regional Water Planning for Sandoval, Bernalillo, Valencia, and Socorro counties. The bill allocated $150,000 to be expended for a cost-sharing agreement with the U.S. Army Corps of Engineers, pursuant to its planning assistance to the state regional water planning program. This money was to be matched by the Corps of Engineers to bring the amount to $300,000 for the project.

I had met with the Army Corps of Engineers a couple of times during the interim between sessions, because of my concern about the water problems of our state's future.

Subas Shah, director of the Middle Rio Grande Conservancy, was interested in the help that the state and the Army Corps of Engineers would provide in mapping and the historical water use in each of the counties.

They all testified to the need for this money, and Representative Pauline Gubbels introduced the bill in the House. It was clear to us that Governor Gary Johnson would follow his rule of vetoing all bills that were new programs and required money. We included the money in House Bill 2 for the state engineer to do regional water studies in the middle Rio Grande basin in fiscal years 1998–1999. This was added in the Senate Finance Committee when we reviewed House Bill 2, which is the state budget bill.

We were able to include money in the budget bill for two of my other bills in the Senate Finance Committee. With the help of Representative Danice Picraux, the UNM nurse-midwifery program was included in the budget for Health Sciences at the University of New Mexico, and the community-based cancer patient support service was included in the Department of Health budget with the help of Senator Billy McKibben.

There are three equal branches of government in our state and our nation. Each of these branches of government has an obligation to share in the distribution of the resources. The three programs I've described above were important and valuable. They were put in the House budget bill, and they were not vetoed. They did not deserve a veto because they were new and innovative. We all have an obligation to evaluate programs that do not accomplish their goals and then eliminate them. But to take a blanket approach of not accepting new ideas because they might cost money is not accepting responsibility for the welfare of the state and its citizens.

One of the major legislative issues on the agenda my first year in the Senate was the Indian Gaming Compact, which had been defeated twice in previous years in the House of Representatives. Once it did pass, the Native American tribes were able to open casinos.

This was a campaign issue, and I had many discussions with members of my district, the two tribes in my district (Santa Ana and Sandia pueblos) and lots of friends. One of the most memorable discussions for me was with a friend from the Santa Ana Pueblo, Roy Montoya, who was the tribal administrator. I asked Roy how gambling would help keep the traditions of the pueblo alive. Roy told me in a very emotional tone of voice, "Pauline we can hardly keep ourselves alive in the poverty a lot of our people live in." He said, "This is one of few ways for our people to get out of poverty and begin to provide money for scholarships for our kids to go to school, develop health clinics on the pueblo, provide mortgages to build houses on our land and provide jobs for our people."

My position was always based on the sovereignty issue, which says that the tribes are sovereign nations, within our states, and they can make decisions to govern themselves. This has not always been interpreted in a uniform way, but for me it was the deciding factor. I was not sure of the consequences for the tribe or the rest of the population, but I thought it was their decision to make. The pueblos wanted the opportunity to have Indian casinos, and I voted yes for the Tribal Compact in the Senate and the final bill that came back from the House.

The capitol was full of lobbyists in favor of gambling and members of the New Mexico Coalition Against Gambling that were opposed. I announced my position and while they did not occupy my office, the issue occupied a lot of time in my committee. To sort through the Senate and House bills, a subcommittee of the Finance Committee was appointed to work with the House to come up with the final language.

The compact term and the amount of money that the state would require back from the casinos were major points of disagreement. The initial Senate bill had a compact term of fifteen years with a five-year renewal. Other issues were that a person had to be twenty-one to gamble or work in the casino, no alcoholic beverages would be allowed at the casino, casinos could not cash paychecks, pension, or government assistance checks. The bill also required background checks for employees and licensing of key casino workers by tribal regulators. The original tax on the casinos was a percentage that was supposed to bring in about $65 million annually to the state. That number seemed to be a moving target, and now, thirteen years later, with further changes in the compact terms and the percentages from the casinos to the state, I have no idea what the amount to the state might be. With our present economic problems I've read that the casinos are not doing as well as in the past.

The pueblos that I represented used their money wisely for the welfare of the members of the tribe during my time in the Senate. The money has changed the power of the pueblos politically, and the configuration of the dollars available for campaigning has also enhanced the tribe's ability to have more influence during the election process.

The Indian Gaming Compacts legislation passed late in the session with a very close vote in the House and it has changed our state. Governor Gary Johnson signed the bill and completed his campaign promise to do so. Depending on who you talk to, it has been good or bad for the state. But, I don't believe we will go back, and we all have to adapt to the change.

CHAPTER SEVENTEEN

The Teaching of Evolution

> It is not the strongest of the species that survives,
> nor the most intelligent that survives.
> It is the one that is most adaptable to change.
> —Charles Darwin

During my first week in the Senate in 1997, I introduced Senate Bill 155, which addressed the teaching of evolution in public schools. I had eight cosponsors, and the drama began as we went from the Senate Education Committee to the floor of the Senate and then to the committees in the House of Representatives.

The single-page bill was to enact a new section of the Public School Code to read:

> Teaching of Evolution—in determining public school curriculum policy or prescribing courses of instruction for public schools, the state board shall adopt curriculum standards for life sciences and earth and space sciences that conform with the National Academy of Sciences' national science education standards for life sciences and earth and space sciences.

This issue became important to parents, teachers, and a majority of students and professors at all of our New Mexico institutions. The reason for the concern was described by physicist David E. Thomas in testimony describing his endorsement of my bill. He said,

> I'm here to endorse the Eisenstadt Evolution Bill. This bill is an essential first step toward the long-term goal of guaranteeing comprehensive and quality science education for the children of New Mexico. The new Science Content Standards, adopted on August 22, 1996, are seriously deficient in several areas, especially those concerning evolution and the age of the Earth. The original writing committee,

composed of science teachers, worked for years on a set of content standards that was released for comments last March. These standards did include evolution and the 4.5-billion-year age of the earth. However, between March and August of last year, these were systematically stripped from the working set of content standards, and are *not* in the version which was finally adopted.

Dave Thomas was speaking for New Mexicans for Science and Reason. He presented a list of other groups that endorsed the legislation including:

The New Mexico Academy of Science, Coalition for Excellence in Science Education, New Mexico Faculty Senate, University of New Mexico Biology Department Faculty, University of New Mexico Biology Department Students, University of New Mexico Earth and Planetary Science Department Faculty, New Mexico Institute of Mining and Technology Faculty Council, New Mexico State University Biology Department Faculty, Staff of the National Solar Observatory, Sacramento Peak, the Society for Integrative and Comparative Biology, and many more groups, private individuals, and clergy.

The list grew to include members of Los Alamos National Lab, staff and managers from Sandia National Laboratories, the Santa Fe Institute, members of church groups, and the rabbi and members of Temple Albert, medical doctors, lawyers, technicians, many teachers, and students.

Prior to the legislative session I conferred with scientists and professors and one of my friends and neighbors who was both, Dr. James S. Findley. Jim was interested in helping to pass this legislation, and he came to Santa Fe to testify in the Senate Education Committee. He was also one of my experts on the floor of the Senate during our two-hour debate along with my friend Kim Johnson, who is a physicist. The news release from our press conference quotes Dr. Findley, former chairman of the University of New Mexico's Department of Biology: "New Mexico's children deserve a modern science education that meets recognized, national standards. Senator Eisenstadt's bill will correct a serious deficiency to the benefit of science students and the rest of us as well."

This press conference was held on January 28, 1997, and that is the day the legislation was introduced. I was quoted in the news release saying, "I feel compelled to challenge the New Mexico State School Board's exclusion of one of the biological sciences from our public school curriculum. This bill would help assure that New Mexico's children will be exposed to modern biology's foundation. I am very concerned about our students and their ability to compete in college and industry if they lack an understanding of the crucial concept of evolution." Dr. Getty of the Coalition for Excellence in Science Education and Dave Thomas were also present at the news conference.

The New Mexico Christian Coalition appeared to lobby at the capitol in 1997. I had never seen them acting as lobbyists during my years in the House of Representatives.

They were very active that year, and they had a legislative summary that was made available to all the members. The summary was about twelve pages long, and it appeared to have about sixty bills that they marked favorable or unfavorable, with a short explanation of why they decided to support or not support legislation.

Senate Bill 155 was described this way in the Christian Coalition 1997 Legislation Summary: "Evolution Only (Not Favored), Introduced by Pauline B. Eisenstadt. This bill, though cloaked in an 'evolution-only' debate is, in fact, a trial balloon for enacting a nation-wide Goals 2000 curriculum, of which requiring the exclusive teaching of the failed theory of evolution is only the tip of the iceberg. Should this effort succeed, New Mexico will lose her education autonomy in favor of a dictatorial and extreme left-oriented central government program. See Appendix A."

In the Christian Coalition's legislative summary, Senate Bill 155 was the only bill that had an appendix, so we investigated appendix A. It was about "Goals 2000," and it was described in the following manner: "Passed in 1994, the Clinton Administration's Goals 2000: Educate America Act is a well-concealed effort to transfer education autonomy from the state and local level, to the national level, where an extreme-left curriculum can be mandated." At the bottom of the page, it says that "Goals 2000 is an all-out war and the targets are marriage, the sanctity of life, the family, the Founding Fathers, Biblical virtues, and even Christ Himself."

I have never understood how my one-page Bill to mandate the use of National Academy of Sciences' national science education standards for life sciences and earth and space sciences would achieve all the things described above. But I did realize that we would be engaged in quite a battle, and we began to organize the scientists as lobbyists. We had no experienced or paid lobbyists, but we had a lot of PhD scientists ready to attend meetings as well as a Nobel Prize winner in physics, Dr. Murray Gell-Mann. The letters from the scientists and the editorials in the newspapers began to arrive in the capitol.

The *Santa Fe New Mexican*, the West's oldest newspaper, founded in 1849, was the first editorial on January 29, 1997, and it nailed the issues from our point of view. The editorial began with the title of, "Taking the Offensive on Evolution's Behalf." It went on to say,

> Ever since the state school board gave short shrift to evolution as it set science-education standards, New Mexico teachers have been looking over their shoulders as they present genetics and other biological knowledge to their students.

Sen. Pauline Eisenstadt-Corrales, has introduced legislation she hopes will get teachers' minds back on science and off religion-politics.

Her bill mandates the teaching of evolution in our state's public schools.

As such, says an impressive lineup of scientists and other academics supporting Eisenstadt's bill, evolution is to biology what math is to algebra: the corner stone of edifice of knowledge.

In New Mexico, you might not know it: A certain spirit of Creationist activism crept into the state's standard-setting process, cutting swaths through pro-evolution guidelines and putting that scientific principle on a back burner.

The standards as drawn so far may be vague enough to allow the stout-hearted to teach evolution, but worrisome enough that some educators skip lightly over the topic—or not at all. And New Mexico youngsters may fare even poorer.

A state like ours, host to two of the world's leading scientific laboratories, needed a legislative champion of this embattled field of science. In Pauline Eisenstadt, we've got one.

She can expect scenes from *Inherit the Wind* in her hallway: The extremists portrayed in the saga surrounding the John Scopes "monkey trial" of 1925 have ideological heirs in late-20th-century New Mexico. They'll be hollering about evolution being rammed down their children's throats and creationism going out the window.

This isn't quite the case: Creationism may merit mention in other classes, and the senator is quick to say so.

She'll have to reassure the Roundhouse's more timid souls on that point and others as she shepherds this bill through the legislature.

This editorial was appreciated because it framed the issue properly for us, as we battled through one committee after another. The editorial page editor was William W. Waters, and I'm sorry I never met him to thank him for his understanding of our battle.

Our battle continued, and it did remind me of *Inherit the Wind*, a movie I had seen many years ago. I had death threats and some very nasty anonymous letters and references to monkey ancestors. The capitol police force were alerted, and they were very good about taking me to committee meetings and guarding the doors to protect against some of the extremist people. The one-page bill generated a lot more activity that I had anticipated. After all, this was not 1925, but here we were fighting for almost seventy-five years of progress in science.

The *Albuquerque Journal* on January 29, 1997, quoted Alan Morgan, state schools superintendent. Morgan said, "The state board did not require that evolution be taught so that teachers are free to include various theories of origin. One of the standards the board adopted requires that students in science be exposed to a variety of theories regarding biological origin to insure that critical thinking and scientific investigation skills be developed." He went on to say, "The strongest fact base is with evolution, but there are many board members who also believe that students need to know there are other beliefs and theories and you have to expose kids to other theories."

In the same *Albuquerque Journal* article supporters of the bill said the exclusion of evolution by the board left public school teachers wondering if the state supported the theory.

A great number of letters came to my office and to members of the Senate Education Committee in support of the bill. The first committee hearing in the Senate Education Committee was scheduled for February 11, 1997.

The files I've kept on this issue took up a full box of my legislative materials, and I've reread them all. The letters of support were from all over the state, and they represented outstanding scientists as well as concerned parents and students. Some were meant to give me courage to continue, a pat on the back, or a bit of humor, and they meant a great deal to me.

Below, I've excerpted some comments from these letters, and I will continue to preserve them for some future battle if they are needed, because they speak eloquently to the issue of teaching evolution.

The first is from Dr. Murray Gell-Mann, a Nobel Prize winner:

> *This is a communication from a New Mexico scientist in support of SB 155. I am a professor and co-chairman of the Science Board at the Santa Fe Institute, having retired some years ago from the R. A. Millikan Professorship at the California Institute of Technology. In 1969 I was awarded the Nobel Prize in Physics for my work on the elementary particles, the building blocks of which all matter is composed.*
>
> *I understand that some so called "creationists" oppose the adoption of the standards in question because they feel that their point of view would not be adequately represented in science classes. It should be emphasized that their ideas, to which they are of course fully entitled, are not science and have no place in natural science classes.*
>
> *Do we want the New Mexicans of the future, when they make decisions about the storage of nuclear waste or the regulation of nuclear power plants, to be trained in "creationist" nuclear physics or in real nuclear physics? De we want the biologists who deal with outbreaks of disease such as the one caused by the Sin Nombre Hantavirus be trained in the "creationist" biology or in real biology?*

Please vote on the side of science, common sense, excellence in education, and a prosperous future for our state. Yours sincerely, Murray Gell-Mann.

Dr. Eugenie C. Scott, director of the National Center for Science Education, wrote a letter entitled "Reasons SB 155 Should Be Passed":

1. *New Mexico students should be able to get the same science education that students in every other state receive using the National Science Education Standards as a guideline.*
2. *National tests like the SATs and ACTs are being revised to reflect the NSES. New Mexico students will be at a disadvantage in competing for college admission if they are not being taught the same material as in other states.*
3. *Defeat of the legislation will be viewed as anti-science, which places New Mexico in a poorer position to compete for conventions and conferences of scientific and technological organizations and societies. Passage of a bill that links New Mexico into a national science education improvement movement would strengthen the idea that New Mexico is a state in which businesses should invest.*

Dr. Alan Hale, director of the Southwest Institute for Space Research and discoverer of the Hale-Bopp comet, wrote,

I regret that my travels associated with my discovery of Comet Hale-Bopp will not permit me to appear in person before you during your hearings on Senate Bill 155. Please accept my appreciation for allowing this appearance by proxy in support of this bill.

It is clear that our society will face immense scientific and technological challenges in the years and decades to come. In order to allow our children to meet these challenges head-on and overcome them, it is imperative that they receive the best scientific education we can give them, which includes the most current knowledge available as well as training in the overall process of how scientific knowledge advances. The last thing we need is for those who face these challenges to be fed unsupported dogmatic assertions and for discredited unscientific ideas from the distant past to be treated on an equal footing with the best scientific knowledge we have today.

The national science education standards devised by the National Academy of Sciences, and the critical thinking skills which are incorporated within them, are the best weapons we can give the next generation to prepare them to deal with the challenges they will face in the next century. As one who cares deeply about humanity's progress into the future, I strongly believe that these standards are an essential part of our children's education, and therefore I strongly support the passage of Senate Bill 155. This will help to ensure New Mexico's continued and well-deserved pre-eminence in scientific discovery, and will allow our children to meet, and overcome, the challenges they will encounter in the years ahead. Sincerely, Alan Hale, PhD, Director.

Mark Boslough, PhD, employee at Sandia Labs, wrote,

In my scientific career, I have never seen so many colleagues agree on anything before. Geologists, physicists, chemists, astronomers, and biologists from throughout the state have all come together in their support of Senate Bill 155, The Evolution Bill. Why do scientists and science educators overwhelmingly support this Bill? Because we think that creationists had a hand in re-writing the current science standards with the intent of subverting science education and turning classrooms into a battleground for their own particular worldview.

Are high school students mature enough to debate "theories" of origins in the classroom? Will the conflict mandated by current standards create a positive, healthy learning environment? Anyone who thinks so should take a good look at how it is being debated in the newspaper letters sections, and on the floor of the legislature.

Surely classroom time is too precious to be wasted on fruitless arguments between science and creationism. Mark Boslough.

A letter from April Holladay stated:

I'm a mother of two children, a citizen of this beautiful state for thirty-nine years, and a scientist—a computer engineer, retired. I beseech you to vote for the Evolution Bill. The legislature is our only hope to rectify omissions in the present state standards. The standards guide the teaching of all our students from kindergarten through high school. Unfortunately, they omit essential science.

Science matters. Our kids matter. They're our future. Our state's national laboratories will need good scientists in the future. Will our kids know enough? Yes! With your greatly needed help. Thanks from the bottom of my heart. Sincerely, April Holladay.

A letter from Marshall Berman said:

I have a PhD in nuclear physics, and have been a practicing scientist for 33 years. I am manager of the Innovative Alliances Department at Sandia National Laboratories, involved in developing partnerships among government, universities and industry.

It is clear that Senator Eisenstadt's bill is not only fundamental to a good science education; it is also fundamental to the Constitutional protection of religious freedom. A group of zealots has demanded that its religious beliefs be taught as science in the state of New Mexico. There is no other issue faced by this Legislature that is more important than the defense of the United States and New Mexico Constitutions' guarantee of separation of church and state and its support of education excellence. This may be the most important bill you have ever considered. Thank you, Marshall Berman.

With all of these support letters, only a few of which I've quoted, we prepared for the appearance at the first committee hearing in the Senate Education Committee. I invited Dave Thomas to sit with me at the table and asked Dr. Jim Findley to testify and also my husband, Dr. Mel Eisenstadt, to present the legal ramifications of the issue. The room was packed, standing room only. The following was reported in the *Albuquerque Journal* the next day, February 12, 1997.

We began our presentation with a description of why we needed this legislation and my concern about our students' ability to compete in the modern high-tech world without an understanding of evolution. My husband, a retired lawyer who also has a doctorate in mechanical engineering, said, "The omission of any reference to evolution in state standards is reminiscent of bills in other states earlier in the century requiring the teaching of creationism. It is an attempt to push an old idea with new words." Citing the *Edwards v. Aguillard* case of 1986, he added that "the federal Supreme Court has ruled that teaching creationism is unconstitutional because it puts religious teachings into law." In that case, the Supreme Court struck down a 1981 Louisiana state law that required "balanced treatment" for the teaching of human origin theories in science classes. On June 19, the court ruled 7–2 against the law that required public schools teaching evolution to teach creation science as well. The court decided that the state law transgressed the separation of church and state because "it seeks to employ the symbolic and financial support of the government to achieve a religious purpose."

Another committee witness, Michael Yates, an Eldorado High School sophomore, described how he wanted to go to college, adding, "I took two biology courses, and neither of them even mentioned evolution. I ended up asking one of the teachers why they didn't mention evolution, and he told me it was because of the parents and the standards. He doesn't want the hassle. If this is a college prep course, it's essential for me to have the proper knowledge of biology. I don't feel I'm getting prepped for college."

Steve Brugge testified,

I am a licensed science teacher at Eisenhower Middle School. Almost every day I tell my 150 students that science is the most important subject in the world—and I sincerely mean this. Senator Eisenstadt's Evolution Bill will assure that teachers have the world's best standards to use when designing lessons. This bill does not dogmatically force curriculum on students, rather it gives a solid, broad outline of what every well-educated person should know. Teachers, too, need world-class standards to protect them from unscientific attacks. As one who has taught evolution as a central part of my curriculum, I can tell you that these standards would have been a welcome support on many occasions.

There were people who spoke against the bill, including Alan Morgan, state schools superintendent. Morgan stated the state school board opposed the bill, as the state legislature should not be mandating that certain theories be adopted for the school curriculum.

A Los Alamos National Laboratory scientist, John Baumgardner said, "The theory of evolution was an 'intellectual fraud' because it does not explain why fossils do not reveal all steps in the evolution of animals from primitive to more complex life forms. The fossil record is deficient." Baumgardner added, "I say evolution is far from fact. I believe the bill is an attack on the religious beliefs of the citizens of New Mexico."

I think that Dr. Timothy Moy, a professor of the history of science at the University of New Mexico, spoke after that. Dr. Moy said,

> Members of both houses have asked whether voting in favor of stronger science teaching is somehow a vote against God or against religion. As a humanities professor and specialist in the history of science, I can tell you that the answer is clearly no. Science and religion are not incompatible; many of the greatest scientists in human history have been deeply religious people. The only time these two ways of making sense of the world come into conflict is when they are forced to intrude upon one another. Sadly, this is precisely what the State Board's science standards now permit, by watering down science teaching for religious reasons, and by opening the door for religious ideas to be taught as science. Adopting the National Standards removes this conflict.

I invited Dr. Moy to testify in the remaining hearings because he had such a nice way with people while getting his point across about the importance of the issue. He was a wonderful resource and I miss his smiling face. Dr. Moy died in an accident a few years ago, and I spoke a bit about his help, in this important effort, at his memorial service.

The bill passed through the Senate Education Committee with a 4 to 3 vote. It was very close, and it became apparent that this would be a difficult task. We then began preparation for the debate on the floor of the Senate, which was six days away.

The debate on the Senate floor lasted for two and half hours, and it wasn't pretty. I had two scientific experts with me to respond to questions, but the questions did not rise to the scientific level. Senator Leonard Lee Rawson, a Republican from Las Cruces, brought a stuffed ape to the Senate floor, and he argued against the scientific veracity of the theory of evolution. He said, "Evolution is not observable." He argued that the Earth is not 4.5 billion years old but only 10,000 years old, one step closer to walking with God. Furthermore, he claimed that with evolution we are one step closer to swinging from the trees.

President Pro Tem Manny Aragon D-Albuquerque said, "To deny the children of this state the teaching of biology and the development of human nature and nature itself is a real mistake. All of a sudden we're here challenging evolution. I'd like to know what happened here. Maybe it's the Diet Coke."

Senate Bill 155 was approved on the floor of the Senate by a 24–17 with a roll call vote. I still have the official roll call sheet in my files. It was primarily a party line vote with two Republicans voting yes and two Democrats voting no. The *Albuquerque Journal* Capitol Bureau had fun with their article the next day. The first paragraph said, "Evolution swung from one limb of the Legislature to another on Monday as the Senate approved a bill that would require the teaching of evolution in public schools and sent it to the House."

We prepared a packet of information containing some of the letters previously quoted from the scientists and the citizens to hand out at the House Business and Industry Committee. The first page was a letter from Gregory Barrette, senior minister at Christ Unity Church. Mr. Barrette, said, "I'm writing as a member of the Christian clergy, in favor of SB155. Not only is the teaching of evolution consistent with the religious beliefs of the majority of the Christian denominations in New Mexico, but last year, evolution became the official and only recognized way to teach the Origin of the Species in the Roman Catholic Church."

We handed out our packets of information, had our speakers make their presentations, and then the members began to express their unhappiness with the bill. It appeared to me that they were looking for reasons to kill the bill. The full committee was not present and they tabled the bill. That almost always means the bill is dead and that is what I thought happened.

I went to see a friend of mine in the House who was a member of the committee, but absent from the meeting that day. I asked him what happened. He was a smart guy, and he knew the value of the bill to the kids and the state. He told me, "Pauline, I know you are right but *your scientists will disappear and the Christian Coalition will kill us in the next election.*" Perhaps my visit had some effect, as the bill was removed from the Business and Industry Committee and sent to the House Education Committee. However, it seemed that the House members were listening to the religious right.

The *Albuquerque Journal* wrote an editorial on February 14, 1997, entitled "Legislature Steps in Where Board Fails." The editorial said, "Without this mandate the fight over evolution falls on the shoulders of public school teachers across the state. It is unconscionable that teachers should bear this burden unsupported by the state board of education. Public school students in New Mexico deserve to be adequately prepared to continue biological studies from the generally accepted groundwork of scientific theory."

We once again testified, with our experts, including Nobel laureate Murray Gell-Mann, and we lost on a vote of 6 to 5 to table the bill.

Greg Toppo wrote in the *Santa Fe New Mexican* on March 27, 1997, that for him the most enduring image from the recent legislative session was the sight of Nobel Laureate Murray Gell-Mann padding out of the House Education Committee hearing room after unsuccessfully urging the committee to consider the importance of the theory called evolution. The title of the column was "Lasting Image: State Thumbs Nose at a Genius."

We lost the battle, but in some ways we won the war. Marshall Berman, one of the scientists, ran for state school board and won with a lot of help from the other scientists. The content standards were eventually changed, and hundreds of scientists were made aware of the importance of political activity. I shared the comment made by my friend in the House, about how the scientists will disappear and not help us in the next election, with my scientist friends. I think it was a lesson learned for them to pay attention to public policy as it affects their lives and work.

It was an experience that I wasn't prepared for in the twentieth century. It will continue to be an issue and the scientists as well as the rest of us need to continue to be vigilant.

My one-page bill addressing the teaching of evolution in 1997 provided me with death threats, a stuffed ape on the floor of the Senate, and a Christian coalition presenting opposition. But I also had a big cheering squad in my district and all around the state.

The late astronomer Carl Sagan compared science to a candle in the dark. My little bill was an effort to strike a match to help the candle burn in New Mexico schools for our children to understand science.

CHAPTER EIGHTEEN

Hate Crimes Legislation

The ultimate measure of a person is not where they
stand in moments of comfort and convenience, but where
they stand in times of challenge and controversy.

—Martin Luther King Jr.

In the official language in which it was given, my hate crimes legislation was an "Act Relating to Criminal Sentencing; Providing Increases in a Basic Sentence of Imprisonment when a Crime is Intentionally Committed against Certain Persons or their Property; Enacting a New Section of the Criminal Sentencing Act."

We have had a law on the books since 1978 that enhances criminal sentencing, and the new material in this legislation added one new category: sexual orientation. The New Material section of the act states, "Non capital Felonies, Misdemeanors, or Petty Misdemeanors against a person or his property because of the actual or perceived race, religion, color, national origin, ancestry, gender, sexual orientation or disability of the person."

If the court or jury finds that an offender committed a misdemeanor or a felony in which a person was intentionally injured or his property was intentionally damaged because of the actual or perceived race, religion, color, national origin, ancestry, gender, sexual orientation, or disability of that person, whether or not the offender's belief or perception was correct, the basic sentence may be increased. The number of days or years of the increase of the sentence of imprisonment varies depending on the offense.

During the late 1990s there was a crime against a gay young man named Matthew Shepherd in Wyoming that stunned the nation. He had been beaten up, tied to a fence, and left to die because he was a homosexual. The revulsion was quick in the gay community nationwide, including New Mexico. But this revulsion was not limited to the gay community, and many of us in the legislature moved forward with our efforts to include the gay and homosexual community in the Hate Crimes Sentencing Law.

When I introduced this bill in 1999 we had almost half of the Senate cosponsoring it with me. Susan Seligman, executive director of the Anti-Defamation League, helped organize the human rights groups and invited them to come and testify to the need for this legislation. Each time we presented this bill, in the Senate Judiciary and the Senate Public Affairs Committees, there was standing room only.

The people came from all over the state to tell their stories about discrimination and the difficulties of living as a gay person. There were young people, old people, parents of gay people, and church people all speaking in favor of this bill. One of the people who helped as my expert witness in committee hearings was Santa Fe district attorney Henry Valdez. He responded to the legal questions in his quiet, competent manner and told the members of the committee how necessary this legislation was for him to prosecute the offenders.

The opposition to this bill continued to follow us as we moved through the process.

They would quote the Bible in their opposition to homosexuality, and claim that "the gay people should get help so they could be normal." The opposition from the Republican members of the Senate was also quite vociferous and lacked compassion for our brothers, sisters, and sons and daughters. One leader said, "A crime is a crime and they should all be punished and we don't have to single out sexual orientation or hate crimes."

We passed the Hate Crimes Sentencing Bill through the Senate with a big majority of the Democrats and a couple Republicans. Senator Don Kidd, a Republican from Carlsbad, was one of those and we became friends.

We continued with the bill in the House of Representatives, and it passed through the House committees in the same ratio as the Senate, a majority of Democrats, and a few Republicans. I went to sit on the floor of the House when this bill was debated and was pleased to see and hear the support of the majority for this bill.

The bill passed both houses, and then of course we had the hurdle of Governor Gary Johnson's possible veto. I asked Senator Don Kidd if he would arrange a meeting with the governor for both of us to talk to him about the need for this legislation, he agreed to make the appointment. He told me that "the governor would meet with us, but not if I was planning to bring the press along with us." I told him I would not do that so our visit was on. The governor listened to us, did not engage in the conversation very much, but he said, "All crimes are hate crimes and we don't need to single some out for enhanced sentencing." We talked about the issues from our point of view, but he vetoed the bill.

The bill passed in 2003 when Governor Bill Richardson became governor. All of the effort on behalf of so many people helped change the climate over time. Changing societal attitudes about acceptable behavior takes a long time. The civil rights movement, the women's movement, and people with disabilities movement have achieved some success in changing behavior in our relationships with each other. The Hate Crimes Legislation was one small effort to help the homosexual community live equal lives and not face discrimination because of their sexual orientation.

CHAPTER NINETEEN

Capital Projects, Sprint Legislation, and Wackenhut

Life grants nothing to us mortals without hard work.
—Horace

The state of New Mexico provides money for projects in the communities around the state in the same way that the federal government does for the states. The process for the distribution of money for projects in our state, during my time in the House and the Senate, was one third for the House, one third for the Senate, and one third for the governor. I know that this has changed, and there is a different formula at the present time. The money comes from severance taxes from oil and gas revenue and general obligation bonds that are voted on by the public. The GO bonds contain money for senior centers, university projects, prisons, large road projects, and other big state projects.

The Senate Finance Committee, which I served on during my time in the Senate, meets and hears the requests from all of the senators. The chairman of the Senate Finance Committee was the late Ben Altamirano. He had a very calm, polite, and pleasant demeanor. Ben presided over the meetings regarding the budget and bills presented by individual members. They were held in the afternoon. The capital project bills came later in the session because we did not know the exact amount of money in the severance tax fund until later in the session. This determined what amount of money was available for each member to allocate to projects in their district.

At that time in the session, Senator Joe Fidel, vice chairman of the Finance Committee, would chair the meetings. Joe had served seven terms, or twenty-eight years, in the Senate and Ben had served eight terms, or thirty-two years, in the Senate. They were experienced leaders, and they treated everyone with respect and kindness, both the people in the audience as well as the senators on the committee. They both served the state of New Mexico well and gave a large part of their lives to public service.

The membership on the Senate Finance Committee changed during my time as people left the committee and new members joined the committee. Senator John Arthur Smith was a co–vice chairman during my last few years, and he helped a lot with getting the bills moving and keeping track of the budget. He is now chairman of the Senate Finance Committee.

When I started in 1997, Senator Manny Aragon was on the committee as were senators Richard Romero and Pete Campos. They left the committee after two years while I was still there. Some of the later senators I served with were senators Leonard Tsosie, Nancy Rodriquez, Sue Wilson, Billy McKibben, and Joe Carraro. The committee reflected the numbers of the majority and minority parties but that is always based on who is present in the committee to vote.

The committee met before the legislative sessions, and about halfway through the session we began to meet all the time. The last ten days we would meet during the evening also, and dinner would be brought into the chairman's office. We'd go in and get a sandwich or they always liked fried chicken. It was a very hardworking committee.

I enjoyed serving on the Senate Finance Committee, because we always knew what the money issues were, which I believe is the major responsibility of the legislature and government. The allocation or saving of resources is the major job of politicians.

The first year of my Senate term, none of us had any capital project money because of Senator Davis's filibuster on the last hour of the last day. Therefore the amount of the money in severance taxes had accumulated and the amount of money available to help our districts was larger than we ever had. We were able to replenish the reserves as well as help all around the state.

Before the session, I would meet with every community in my district and request their priorities for legislative help. I met with the mayors and councilors of Rio Rancho, Corrales, the town of Bernalillo, Sandoval County, and residents of my little unincorporated communities like Placitas, Cedar Crest, and Sandia Park. The cities and towns would have lists of their needs, but it was more difficult to get a consensus in the unincorporated areas.

The commentary I wrote after the legislative session describes the projects I was able to fund in 1998. The following are excerpts from the commentary in the *Rio Rancho Observer*:

Rio Rancho Loma Colorado municipal park, $70,000; Rio Rancho park rehabilitation, $50,000; Sabana Grande pool, $50,000; Rio Rancho ambulance, $40,000; Rio Rancho library, $25,000; Corrales Loma Larga Road, $100,000; Corrales Elementary School, $35,000;

Rio Rancho school textbooks, $50,000; Sandoval County domestic violence shelter, $40,000; Bernalillo Community Center, $150,000; New Mexico War Museum, $20,000; Bernalillo Roosevelt Library, $100,000; Carroll Elementary School playground, $50,000; Cibola High School technology, $50,000; Placitas Open Space, $50,000; and Vista Grande Community Center in Sandia Park, $25,000.

The requests from my district totaled more than $4 million, and I was able to pass legislation for about one-fourth of that amount. I met one of our new legislators at a county Democratic convention in April 2010, and he said how lucky I was when there was money for local projects. He said, "Nobody even comes to my office in Santa Fe to see me because I have no pork money to help with their projects." The economy was good during most of my years in Santa Fe.

From 1999 to 2000, I was able to help with the needs of the communities in my district by getting about $300,000 in two years for phase one of the Corrales sewer system, which the Village of Corrales began in 2010. Some additional funding for the following projects was obtained during those years: Casa San Ysidro Museum improvements, $10,000; Corrales Elementary School wetlands, $45,000; Algodones Elementary School playground improvement, $25,000; and other projects similar to the ones listed above.

Some of my legislative friends in the House told me that the pork projects were the reason they came to Santa Fe, to help their little towns and rural areas. The money to help with these projects is not available from general fund budgets and during times of economic stress these projects and needs are not met.

When I drive through my former district now, I always remember the effort we put into getting the help for these roads, schools, libraries, community centers, and other projects. All of the projects required meetings before the session, people coming to Santa Fe to testify and bring data, arranging schedules, answering questions in the committee, and following up. It still puts a smile on my face when I see kids using a soccer field or baseball field, community centers, and the like that I helped bring to our communities.

Sprint Legislation: 1998 Senate Bill 204

In 1998, I sponsored a bill titled Accounting and Administrative Services Deduct, which was the enabling legislation for Sprint PCS, a limited partnership, to locate a call center in Rio Rancho. The center was a subsidiary of telecommunications giant Sprint Corporation and would bring twelve hundred jobs paying an average of $35,000 a year with benefits. Sprint would invest $4 million to build the center and the yearly payroll was anticipated to be $40 million.

○ Announcement of Sprint's location in Rio Rancho. Pauline at the podium, Governor Gary Johnson on the left, and Mayor John Jennings on the right. Other legislators in the background.

The bill was necessary to correct a state tax law inequity and encourage the company to expand operations in New Mexico. This project required that we expand a gross receipts tax deduction to cover certain limited partnerships. The current deduction waives taxes on transactions between a company and its affiliates, but it covers such arrangements only between corporations, not limited partnerships.

In February 1998, I received a letter from Sprint spokeswoman Sheryl Wright, in which she wrote that "the current tax inequity is a critical roadblock to Sprint and our affiliated company Sprint PCS in selecting a site. New Mexico has been at the top of our business plan list for the call center because of its strong labor force and the people's quality work ethic."

Noreen Scott, executive director of the Rio Rancho Economic Development Corporation, said that "she believed two other states were in the running but she didn't have further information."

This legislation seemed like a win-win situation with 1,200 jobs, high average wage of $35,000, annual payroll of $40 million, and the bill was to expand the current tax deduction between corporations to include limited partnerships. I waited eagerly for my bill to be scheduled so I could arrange for the Sprint PCS Company to send their people to Santa Fe to testify.

After three or four days I asked Senator Carlos Cisneros, who was chairing the Ways and Means Committee (where all the tax related bills were referred), "When will my Sprint Bill be scheduled in your committee?" Carlos sat next

⊙ Pauline with Sheryl Wright, spokeswoman for Sprint. In the background
are Senator Richard Romero, left, and Governor Gary Johnson on the right
extending a handshake.

to me on the floor of the Senate, and he told me, "It is not going to be heard."
After I made further inquiry, he told me to talk to Manny.

I prepared all of my data, made copies of all the related facts concerning
the bill that described the benefits, and went to the next Democratic caucus
meeting to argue my case.

Manny indeed did not want to have this bill scheduled, and he asked that
I bring into the caucus Mr. O'Neil, the deputy director of taxation to further
explain the bill. I did that and he explained the impact of this bill, until there
were no more questions and he left.

I went through the job benefits, the payroll, and the investment to the
state again and then Senator Manny Aragon said, "Pauline those jobs aren't
going to the South Valley, are they?" I said, "No Manny, they are not, but
your people can get in their cars and drive twenty minutes and they can have
those jobs."

It was quiet in the room, and then from one side and the other I heard,
"Let her have it, Manny." "Give it to her." That is the back story about how we
got enabling legislation to help locate the Sprint call center in Rio Rancho,
New Mexico.

The Wackenhut Issue

An article in the *Santa Fe New Mexican* written by Mark Oswald in June 14,
1998, brought to the public's attention an issue that had been of great concern

to many of us in the Senate. The article described a Saturday morning caucus called to discuss Senator Manny Aragon's new consulting contract with Wackenhut Corrections. About Senator Aragon the article said, "He made it very clear that he would abstain from voting on any measures involving private prison operator Wackenhut Corrections. But he wouldn't abstain from voting on the state government budget." Senator Cisco McSorley, who had called for Aragon to give up the Wackenhut job or step down from the powerful position of president pro tem, denied comment on Saturday's discussion.

After the meeting, I told the press that "I expressed my concerns to Senator Aragon. I'm hoping he will reconsider doing the consulting job for Wackenhut while he's president of the Senate."

The conflict of interest issue was written all over this situation. Senate rules don't outright prohibit members from taking jobs with contractors of companies dependent on state funding, but there is language laying bare Aragon's conflict: "A senator shall not accept or engage in employment if the senator knows it is being afforded him with the intent to influence his conduct in the performance of his official duties."

The drumbeat from the media continued about this situation, and finally I called Manny and told him that the next time the media called me about this issue, I would tell them what I've already told him. "That he can't continue as president of the Senate and have a consulting contract with Wackenhut as they are building prisons for the state in both Hobbs and Santa Rosa. He should choose between the consulting contract or the presidency of the Senate." About six weeks later Manny called to tell me that he had decided that I and some of the others were right and he gave up his contract.

The need for clear lines of conflict of interest, an ethics commission, and legislative ethics reform was once again center stage. The public loses trust in the process, the legislature, and politics when these kinds of conflicts continue to exist.

On March 18, 2009, Senator Manny Aragon, was sentenced to five and half years in prison. He pleaded guilty to three federal felony counts of conspiracy and mail fraud in a scheme to defraud the state of nearly $4.4 million in the construction of the Bernalillo County Metropolitan Courthouse in Albuquerque. He broke down with emotion and expressed sorrow and apologized to his family and New Mexicans.

This was nine years after I had retired from the Senate, but I had voted on the money for the Metropolitan Courthouse because Senator Aragon had told us that it was needed. I think the project was needed, but the price was bloated by the $4.4 million that he and his partners in crime skimmed off the top for themselves.

My emotional response to this outrage was one of betrayal by Manny combined with sorrow for him and his family. He always reminded me of the legendary Navajo figure called the shapeshifter. The same idea is used in *Star Trek*. A shapeshifter changes to fit the environment or needs of the situations. Manny could change to become charming, humorous, or angry if the situation needed that response. He was one of the smartest men in the Senate, and he accomplished a lot of great things for the state and his district.

I think he lost his way, and I expect he will use his extraordinary leadership skills in prison to organize his prison mates to get better food in the cafeteria or more books in the library. When he has paid his debt to society, I hope he can once again become the good man he once was.

CHAPTER TWENTY

Telecommunications Legislation and Retirement

The very essence of leadership is that you have a vision.
—Theodore Hesburgh

It was becoming quite clear to me in 1998 that the development of the Internet and the whole area of telecommunications was an essential part of the future in our state, country, and world. I was on economic development committees for the National Conference of State Legislatures when the discussions about international Internet polices were the top priority.

The business community in New Mexico was supporting the creation of a bipartisan Internet Caucus in the New Mexico legislature. It was to be part of the United States Internet Council. William Myers, CEO of the United States Internet Council, came to New Mexico and described to us the idea of legislatures throughout the United States discussing the policy issues surrounding this new commercial medium. Intel Corporation, which was the major employer in my district and the state, was very supportive of the creation of the United States Internet Council. Barbara Brazil, director of public affairs for Intel Corporation, introduced me to William Meyers and indicated that she thought this might be an important vehicle to help our state overcome the problems of the "digital divide."

The president of the Senate appointed me to serve as Senate democratic cochair of the New Mexico Internet Caucus. His letter of appointment stated, "Senator Pauline Eisenstadt has a good working relationship with the local business community and is knowledgeable about Internet issues."

I attended the United States Internet Council Steering Committee meeting in Washington, DC, that year, representing New Mexico. It was a useful network of legislators who were interested in helping our states prepare for the dramatic changes the Internet would make in our future world. We could not imagine what the world economy would look like ten years later, but we all knew it would not be the same.

One of my major objectives during the remaining years of my Senate term was to highlight for our state legislature the need to help New Mexicans participate in this new economy. On January 24, 2000, I had prepared a news release that read as follows: "Santa Fe –Senator Pauline B. Eisenstadt, D-Corrales, will be joined by other legislators and representatives of the business community at a news conference at 2:00 p.m. on Thursday, January 27th in the Capitol Rotunda to discuss a legislative package of telecommunications bills designed to help bridge the 'digital divide' in New Mexico." On the appointed day, we had prepared handouts with our remarks. The rotunda was crowded with bipartisan legislators, the business community, and lots of lobbyists and citizens. We had a platform set up, with microphones, and we began the discussion.

Calling the "digital divide" a threat that separates New Mexicans into information "haves" and "have-nots," our bipartisan group of lawmakers announced its intention to bridge the divide with a package of legislative measures that session.

The legislators had the support of the business community, the broadband coalitions, and the governor's science advisor. The cornerstones of our program were to create a state telecommunications council, replace the "rate of return" pricing policy with price caps, create a telecommunications infrastructure fund, and enact a telecommunications consumer's Bill of Rights. "These changes were designed to make advanced telecommunications more accessible to all New Mexicans," I said, as one of the chief sponsors of the package.

"Information networks today are like the highways of the last century that were so critical to our country's prosperity. They are the foundations of economic growth and are critical to improving education and health care," I said during a news conference at the state capitol. At the news conference, Senator Roman Maes of Santa Fe seconded these ideas, saying, "We must move forward to develop the economy of New Mexico. This legislative effort will help us do that."

"The good news is that more New Mexicans, both at home and at work, are using computers and the Internet to access rich information resources and to create new, innovative businesses," said Representative Rhonda King, D-Stanley.

"The bad news is that the digital divide between the information rich and the information poor is large and it may be widening. At this time in our history when broadband, high-speed telecommunications capabilities are the keys to the future, too many New Mexicans are falling through the net," I said. "We must provide the incentives to providers of broadband, high-speed telecommunications access so that all New Mexicans can participate in the global economy and electronic commerce."

"It is critical that as more and more New Mexicans are using computers at work, at school and at home that the infrastructure be in place to not
only support those computers but to make the most of their potential," said
Representative Rob Burpo, R-Albuquerque.

"Telecommunications reform is one of the actions we can take in Santa Fe
that can have a tangible, long-lasting and, most importantly, positive impact
on people's lives," said Senator William H. Payne, R-Albuquerque.

The digital divide impacts a state like New Mexico disproportionately
because of the state's rural nature and its demographics. The U.S. Department
of Commerce recently found that households in rural areas are less likely to
have computers and access to the Internet than households in urban areas or
in cities. Households at certain income levels are also less likely to be connected. And for certain groups, including Hispanics and Native Americans,
problems of low telephone penetration and Internet connectivity are espe-
cially acute.

Some of the legislative measures to address the digital divide that we considered in the House and Senate during the 2000 session included:

- The creation of the New Mexico Telecommunications
  Council (Senate Bill 124) to coordinate the many public and
  private efforts to improve telecommunications capabilities in
  the state and to ensure that New Mexico develops forward-
  looking, sound policies
- The elimination of the rate of return pricing for telecommunications services and a return to a reasonable price cap system
  (Senate Bill 123)
- The establishment of a telecommunications infrastructure
  development fund to address some of the critical unmet needs
  of New Mexico's communities (Senate Bill 181)
- A telecommunications consumer's Bill of Rights (Senate Bill 115)
  to protect consumers from abuses on the part of telecommunications providers
- Funding for an assessment of the state's information infrastructure (Senate Bill 116)

There was one more bill that I introduced with Senator Roman Maes for
the Economic and Rural Development and Telecommunications Committee
(Senate Bill 100). This bill was directed to the economic development secretary. The bill directed the secretary to contract a service that provides for state
websites at no cost, to establish an online portal to an electronic commerce
marketplace, and that pays a rebate to the state on all sales made by businesses
in the electronic commerce marketplace when those businesses are contacted

through the online portal on the state's website. Revenues from the rebate were to be deposited in the educational technology fund.

About halfway through the news conference Senator Manny Aragon came running over to me with a blue telephone message paper. I was on the podium in the middle of the discussion of our bills when he handed it to me. The note said, "Your husband has been taken to the Heart Hospital in Albuquerque." This stopped me in midsentence, and I told Roman Maes what had happened and gave him the microphone and stepped down from the podium.

I looked at the audience and saw my friend Marlene Feuer, the statewide president of Waste Management. I went over to where she was standing and told her what had happened and asked for her help. She immediately agreed to go with me to my office, then to the condo to get some overnight stuff and follow me to the hospital in Albuquerque. We left the rotunda and headed to the fourth floor, where my office was located. As we got off the elevator, Manny came huffing up the stairs to the fourth floor and stopped me. He said, "You left so fast I didn't get a chance to talk to you. How can I help you? What can I do? Do you need a ride to Albuquerque?" I told him Marlene was going to help me and I would call him later and let him know what was happening.

I write this now to demonstrate one of Manny's other sides, the endearing and genuine caring side that made him so beloved by the senators he worked with in the legislature. I had challenged him and didn't always agree with him, but I was one of his family members as a state senator and I was having a big problem. He wanted to be there for me in my time of need. I continue to have mixed emotions about Manny and hope he will find some peace during the rest of his life.

We got to the hospital and Marlene's husband Steve Feuer had already arrived to help. My husband Mel had a mild heart attack, and he was in surgery where they were opening up an artery and installing a stent. He was very lucky. There was no heart damage, and Dr. Barry Ramo, his doctor, said he would be fine. I spent the next two nights in the Heart Hospital with him and we went home.

I asked our younger son, Keith, to come to Albuquerque to help with Mel's recovery, and fortunately he was able to leave his work in Washington, DC. Keith stayed for a week and that allowed me to get back to finish the legislative session.

The telecommunications bills did not fare so well, but we knew that might happen as all but one had appropriations, and they had to get in line with all the other requests for money. My Senate Bill 100 to contract for electronic commerce services to generate revenue for an educational technology fund passed through both houses, but was vetoed by the governor.

We had a vision of what was needed and we tried to do something about it, but it was too soon. We did educate the legislators, and over time I hope some of our plans to meet the needs of the state on these issues will be realized.

Retirement

In March 2000, I announced that I would retire from the Senate and my service in the House and the Senate came to an end. I felt deep gratitude to the people I worked with in Santa Fe, who helped me achieve some good things and feel that my time was well spent. I will always remember with great fondness many of the senators and House members that I worked with over the years. One of the best things about serving in the legislature is the opportunity to get to know and befriend people from all corners of our beautiful state. When we drive through the state, I remember my friends who live in those areas, the battles we had, and the issues we agreed on. I've tried to describe some of these so that you, the reader, can understand how my corner of the Roundhouse functioned for me.

The staffs of the Legislative Council; the late Margaret Larragoite, the Senate clerk, and her staff; as well as all of the competent people who work in our state agencies make the jobs of the elected officials possible. The last Senate secretary I worked with was Elaine Sullivan. She was a lifesaver on many occasions, and she and her husband Bernie have remained good friends, as have many of my other secretaries from the legislative sessions.

There were also many lobbyists that I worked with over my dozen years. Some of the ones I found to be most helpful were Bill Garcia, Marie Eaves, Joe Menapace, Dan Najar, Charlie Marquez, Mary Sue Gutierrez, and Neal Gonzales. The nonprofit lobbyists were also most helpful on the children's issues of child abuse and prenatal care. Then, of course, there were the educational lobbyists of the school districts, higher education, and the teacher's unions. Lobbyists are a part of the mix that makes the process work. One has to discriminate about the lobbyists that will tell you both sides of the story and be honest with you and those who won't.

It was ironic to me that I had made the decision to retire from politics for a lot of reasons, but my health was fine, so I thought. On Halloween night, October 31, 2000, I was rushed to the Heart Hospital with a blocked artery. It was my husband's turn to sleep in the chair during my two nights in the hospital as they had put a stent in my artery also. I have accused him of having a contagious heart problem. Dr. Ramo, who now became my doctor too, assured me that there was no heart damage and with an aspirin and Lipitor I would be fine.

It is ten years later, and we are both doing well, but our lives have dramatically changed. I no longer shoulder the responsibility for everyone in my district. I tried to address the problems that I thought needed to be confronted, and this commitment involved a lot of stress. Public service is time consuming and rewarding at the same time, but there is a time and a season for all the challenges in our lives, and it was time for me to move on to my next season.

CHAPTER TWENTY-ONE

Life After Politics

The real voyage of discovery consists not in seeking
new landscapes, but in having new eyes.
—Marcel Proust

*T*echnology Talks is an idea that I had been working on for quite awhile. After I retired from the Senate, I put a lot of time into the idea of a *Technology Talks* television program, because I was concerned about the many changes taking place. I hoped that more New Mexico policymakers would be involved and that the citizens of our state would share in benefits of the revolution taking place in information technology.

KNME-TV, Channel 5, agreed to produce the show if I helped with the funding for the six-part series and I did. Funding for the show was provided in part by America Online, Intel Corporation, Lectrosonics, and Qwest.

A news release from KNME described *Technology Talks* as a "six-part series produced by Pauline Eisenstadt (former NM State Senator) and KNME-TV that will present Southwest, national, and global information technology issues and discuss policy issues that are relevant to New Mexicans." *Technology Talks* was nonpolitical and informative, allowing New Mexicans to envision participating in the new economy. It aired on Friday evenings at 8:00 p.m., premiering July 6, 2001.

I wanted to produce this show because I felt that the world had changed and there were no electronic borders. People all over the world can be in touch with each other to do business, send e-mails, and the like. Technology knows no geographical boundaries. However, I thought people were using technology without thinking through what's happening with it. There were many issues of concern. I wanted people to begin to understand that it was not just simply about turning on your computer and going to work. What if that computer invades someone's medical or financial privacy? What is being done about crime on the Internet?

Technology Talks also looked at ways of helping long-distance/digital education. I also examined the sharing of medical procedures in rural areas, the discounting of prices via electronic commerce, e-mail throughout the world, as well as electronic government. These advances bring tremendous promise for the future and great challenges to our system of government.

I wanted to look at finances and government too. If electronic commerce was limiting a city or state's gross receipts tax because electronic purchasers paid taxes at the point of origin, this was an issue that needed to be explored. It is an example of how public policy can impact everyday lives. Do taxes need to be restructured? Should we vote on the Internet as some states, such as Arizona, do already?

Technology Talks presented a series of informative topics and took a look at different sides of the issues. I wanted to provide some possible solutions that could then be enacted in the political arena. I hoped to provoke discussion in these areas with these particular shows.

We had participants on the show from Washington, DC, whom I had worked with when I served on national committees. These included Paul Russinoff, director of state public policy for America Online/Time Warner; William Meyers, CEO, United States Internet Council; and Senator Scott Howell of Utah, a manager with IBM. Some of the local people we got on the show were John Badal, vice president, Qwest of New Mexico; Bill Garcia, manager of public affairs, Intel; Jim Hall, CEO, Oso Grande Technologies; Ed Lopez Jr., former V.P. of U.S. West New Mexico; Randy Burge, CEO, New Mexico Information Technology and Software Association; Robert Salazar, former director, Office of Science and Technology, state of New Mexico; Steve Sanchez, director of educational technology; Marilyn Morgan, former president, League of Women Voters, Albuquerque; and many other participants.

The topics we discussed each week were "The Global Economy," "Power of the Microchip," "Taxes on the Internet?," "Privacy on the Internet," "Consumer versus the Net," and "Electronic Government."

This was a big effort for me because I was scheduling all the participants, doing the fundraising, writing the scripts, and preparing the topics. Besides being aired on Friday evenings from July 6 through August 10, the show was repeated on Sunday mornings, and then there was a repeat of the whole series. The comments were terrific and we developed quite a following for the series. It was also streamed over the Internet.

When it was concluded, KNME was interested in continuing the series, but they also needed me to continue doing the fundraising. At that time, my life took another direction, and I decided not to do another series. I very much enjoyed this exploration of the Internet technology and the needs for the public and policymakers to adapt to the massive changes in our world.

✪ On board ship, cruising the Caribbean. Mel was the author on board.

In March 2010, Apple introduced a new computer, the iPad, which competes with the laptop, but it only weighs one and a half pounds and does not need a mouse. Our fingers do all the walking or touching on the screen. I'm also waiting for the voice activated small computer that I can carry around with me and I expect it will happen soon. The opportunities for countries without networks of landlines to come into the global economy are now possible because of Internet technology and cell phones. The innovations continue, and New Mexico is on the ground floor because of our national labs and our universities.

My husband Mel has been writing and publishing novels about energy, environmental, and political issues. He has written four novels: *Navajo Afterglow*, *Noah's Millennium*, *The Dynamite Campaign*, and *The Great Colorado River Water War*. His novels became the reason that we began to travel all over the world on cruise ships for about seven years, taking one or two cruises yearly. He was invited to become an "enrichment specialist" and the author on board the ships.

He gave lectures on writing and his novels as we traveled as guests of the cruise lines. We traveled to Alaska, Europe, the Scandinavian capitals, Mexico, Hawaii, and many times to the Caribbean. It was a bountiful way to travel on the

⚬ Family reunion celebrating our fiftieth wedding anniversary in 2010. Front row left to right: Spencer Eisenstadt, Holly Eisenstadt, Pauline, Mel, Paola Eisenstadt, and Natalia Eisenstadt. Back row left to right: Kristy Pilgrim Eisenstadt, Keith (Keegan) Eisenstadt, Todd Eisenstadt, and Mireya Solis Eisenstadt. Courtesy of Portait Innovations.

⚬ Alaskan cruise with my sister Mickey and brother-in-law Sid Greenspan for their fiftieth anniversary. Left to right: Austin Payne, Mel, Pauline, Sid, Mickey, Tristan Payne, Brandon Kaufer, Laurel Kaufer, Zach Kaufer, Sherra Payne, and Todd Payne.

✪ Grandchildren begin
to arrive: Keith, Kristy,
and Spencer.

✪ Keith and Kristy's baby
daughter Holly Miel.

high seas; we ate well, met some great people, participated in the activities on
board, and visited a lot of exotic places for the first time. We met other enrichment people who taught bridge, golf, and one couple gave Samba lessons. We
continue to correspond with some of the people we met during those trips.

We now have four grandchildren and a lot of our travels are to visit them in
Bethesda, Maryland, or Missoula, Montana. Todd and his wife Mireya and two
daughters, Natalia and Paola, live in Bethesda where they both are professors of
political science at American University. Our son Keith and his wife Kristy and
their children, Spencer and Holly, live in Missoula. Keith has an environmental

○ Todd, Mireya, Natalia, and little Paola.

business called Clear Sky Climate Solutions, and Kristy is a geneticist for the National Parks Department and manages a laboratory that specializes in DNA analysis of endangered species at the University of Montana.

We've arranged family reunions at wonderful places for the last four years—Yellowstone National Park, Glacier National Park, a Mexican cruise, and Myrtle Beach in South Carolina. The children all play together, and we get to be doting grandparents. In 2010, they all came back to Corrales, New Mexico, for our family reunion, and we went to all of our favorite places in New Mexico, of which there are many. The year 2010 was also special as we celebrated our fiftieth wedding anniversary.

We still like to take big river trips in Europe and often go with our friends Bettye and Jack Bobroff. Age changes what is appealing for travel plans, and we are beginning to like driving trips nearby.

Politics still captures my attention, and I jump into situations where I can help by using my particular skill set. That skill set includes knowing the elected officials for a couple of generations. That means I can call them and get an answer or help with a community problem. One of these problems was the survival of Casa San Ysidro, the colonial Hispanic museum in Corrales. Albuquerque mayor Marty Chávez indicated that he wanted to disband the collection, take the farm implements to the Biological Park, and sell the land. There was uproar in the Village of Corrales, and many people seemed to think that it was too late to save it.

○ Our world traveling friends, Bettye and Jack Bobroff.

There was a big community meeting in the old church building organized by Taudy Smith, which I attended. I indicated that I was willing to help organize a group to help save the Casa San Ysidro Museum. A number of us set out to do just that. We formed a group called Save Casa San Ysidro Museum and collected petitions, some money, and formulated a plan to have multimanagement between the Village of Corrales, Sandoval County, and the Albuquerque Museum. Mayor Chávez and I had served in the legislature together, but he was not changing his mind, and I was not successful at first in convincing him to not destroy our colonial Hispanic museum.

We developed a steering committee for the group and met regularly for about four months to plan our campaign. The members of the steering committee were Patrick McNertney, Michelle Frechette, Pat Clauser, Roma Arrellano, and myself. We went to meetings, made presentations, and got one big anonymous donation offer for fifty thousand dollars. The key turning point was at a meeting with Governor Bill Richardson. We went to meet the governor with village officials, county officials, a museum board foundation member, and old friends of Bill's former congressional district. The governor was interested in helping us save the museum. At one point he said, "Pauline, would $200,000 help?" Everyone sitting in his conference room clapped.

The museum still exists today, but we always need more visitors, and if you haven't seen this jewel of historical significance, please visit.

About six years ago, I began to take art classes in Corrales. An artist friend of mine, Michaela Karni, suggested I try a watercolor class in the neighborhood taught by Sylvia Gormley. It was my first time trying to do watercolor painting and I liked it. There is a freedom to watercolor as the paint flows on the paper, sometimes by itself, making very nice combinations of color and shapes. I've painted the Sandia Mountains pink, yellow, purple, and shades of red. I've moved the mountains to suit my paintings and loved every minute of it. After a while, I wanted to try oil painting and I began by painting with the palette knife, but then later switched to the brush. My oil painting teacher is Patty Kruger. Both of my teachers have given me an appreciation of color, shapes, perspective, and the joy of painting.

I've sold original paintings, prints, cards of my paintings, and had commissions to be a house painter. This was fun, as I painted the outsides of houses in Corrales on canvas not on walls. Primarily, we attend arts and crafts shows in Corrales or have studio art tours at our home and sell my paintings, my husband's novels, and his jewelry.

There are two restaurants that have my prints for sale, one in Corrales, the Indigo Crow, and one in Bernalillo, the Prairie Star. I'm the "bathroom queen" at the Indigo Crow as that is where they display my prints. At first, I asked, "When do I graduate to the restaurant?" But they seem to sell well there, and it has become a family joke. When a print is sold, I take my husband out to dinner at that restaurant. We have eaten well on a number of occasions.

As I began to paint I met many talented people who did arts and crafts in Corrales, and it became apparent to me that a venue for the artists to sell their work to the public was needed. I knew that there was a Santa Fe Society of Artists and that they held frequent arts and crafts shows in a bank parking lot in Santa Fe. After talking to one of their officials, who kindly sent me a copy of their bylaws, we began to think about starting a Corrales Society of Artists. We altered their bylaws to suit our community and established a Founding Committee. We had our eye on the library park, La Entrada Park, as a venue for Art in the Park events. We talked with Corrales mayor Gary Kanin, and the Village Council. I then asked the late councilor Bob Bell to sponsor legislation enabling our Corrales Society of Artists to be sponsored by the Parks and Recreation Department. The necessity for this was the need to be covered by the village insurance.

The village was supportive of our efforts and Pat and Jay Norman became the driving force for the Corrales Society of Artists, and Art in the Park continues today, about five years later. There have been many changes, but the event occurs from May through October on the third Sunday of the month.

Each event hosts forty to fifty artists working in media such as painting, sculpture, ceramics, fiber art, and jewelry. Food and entertainment are available as well. Parking and admission are free. My husband and I participated

⊛ Pauline's painting "Dixon Road" in Corrales, watercolor.

⊛ "Apple Blossom Time" in Corrales, oil painting.

in the beginning events, but our travel schedule conflicted with our continued participation. The time was ripe for the creation of this artist society and the Art in the Park events. It was a project that I helped get started, but it would not have continued if the need were not here. We continue to support the efforts of the Corrales Society of Artists.

There are many nonprofit boards that I continue to serve on such as the Rio Rancho Rotary Foundation Board, Anti-Defamation Board, the Musical Theatre Southwest (for two years), Jewish Community Center Board, the Citizens for Casa San Ysidro, and I continue to serve on the State Central Committee for the Democratic Party for Sandoval County and the state of New Mexico.

The new University of New Mexico west campus in Rio Rancho had their grand opening in April 2010, and I've worked with Dr. Beth Miller to help establish a Community Advisory Council for the new campus. This new campus in the City Center will help the community become an educational leader in the state of New Mexico.

The Corrales Book Club is a group of women friends that I enjoy meeting with and discussing the books that we have read. We meet on a monthly basis, and I've read books that have been selected that would not have been on my list of choices, but I found new topics to enjoy discussing.

Life after politics has given me the opportunity to explore new interests, work in new areas of the community, and meet new challenges for the latter part of my life.

Politicians need to pay close attention to the time in their lives when it is good to retire and move on to new challenges. I have watched many of my colleagues stay too long. They lose their eagerness to try new solutions, they are less likely to be innovative or creative because it requires a lot of energy and hard work. I do not think that term limits would be a good answer. Each of us, as an elected official, needs to honestly analyze when it is time to step aside and let another pair of eyes and ears help to solve the problems of our communities.

Power is the ultimate aphrodisiac, it has been said, and I have seen it in action. It is always temporary, and we all need someone to make sure we remember that. In ancient Rome, when the conquering generals came home victorious, they were given a magnificent parade in the Roman coliseum. There was always a person in the chariot with the general, whose job it was to repeat over and over in the general's ear, "Thou art Mortal, Thou art Mortal."

Index